THE BATHROOM
COMPANION

Copyright © 2005
by James Buckley Jr.

All rights reserved. No part of
this book may be reproduced in
any form without written permis-
sion from the publisher.

Library of Congress Cataloging in
Publication Number: 2004111739

ISBN: 1-59474-028-3

Printed in Singapore
Typeset in Century, Officina
Designed by Bryn Ashburn

Illustrations by Wendy Smith
Distributed in North America by
Chronicle Books
85 Second Street
San Francisco, CA 94105

10 9 8 7 6 5 4 3 2

Quirk Books
215 Church Street
Philadelphia, PA 19106
www.quirkbooks.com

THE BATHROOM COMPANION

A COLLECTION OF FACTS ABOUT THE MOST-USED ROOM IN THE HOUSE

BY JAMES BUCKLEY JR.

QUIRK BOOKS
PHILADELPHIA

In 1596, Sir John Harrington invented the first modern flushing toilet. Queen Elizabeth I, Harrington's god-mother, called for one to be installed in her home, but the smell kept her from using it. Alexander Cummings's 1775 invention of a U-shaped bend in the piping helped keep the smell from backing up (usually), but even with that, the flush toilet was years away from popularity. (Thomas Crapper was a Victorian-era plumber, but he did not invent the toilet.)

....

DON'T BELIEVE EVERYTHING YOU READ

On December 28, 1917, the *New York Evening Mail* published a satirical piece by famed humorist H. L. Mencken. The story, called "A Neglected Anniversary," purported to be a history of the plumbed bathtub in America. Mencken wrote at length about a man named Adam Thompson, who viewed an early tub in England and was determined to introduce it to Americans. The writer went on to describe physicians' vehe-ment protestations to this newfangled item and the instal-lation of the first bathtub in the White House, ordered by President Millard Fillmore.

Mencken never suspected that readers would take the story seriously. But it was pretty dry humor, and soon his faux reporting showed up in legitimate articles, essays, and even scholarly journals. By 1926, it had gone so far that Mencken wrote a retraction, "Melancholy Reflections," which a number of newspapers syndicated. Three weeks later the *Boston Herald* used some of the original misinformation in a serious news piece.

Even after Mencken published yet another retraction, this one also widely syndicated, his tongue-in-cheek history seemed to maintain a life of its own.

The first bathroom, but not the first toilet, was built in the Palace of Knossos on Crete in about 1700 B.C. Archaeologists discovered a simple gravity-run system that moved water through the area below the privy hole, cleaning the area after each use in a flushlike manner. The pipes were not long, solid lengths, but rather linked, tapered sections that helped the water flow more quickly. A large terracotta tub was also uncovered on the island. Nearly five feet (1.5 m) long, it had notches for a crossbar on which might have rested bathing implements.

TOP ★10★

TOOTHPASTE BRANDS IN THE U.S.

1. Crest	6. Rembrandt
2. Colgate	7. Sensodyne
3. Aquafresh	8. Listerine
4. Mentadent	9. Closeup
5. Arm & Hammer	10. Ultrabrite

The first toothbrush with bristles was developed in China in 1498. Bristles were taken from hogs at first and later from horses and even badgers. Not until 1938 were nylon bristles—more sanitary and less dangerous—developed by DuPont.

MOVIE SCENES IN BATHROOMS

THE GODFATHER (1972)
Young Michael Corleone (Al Pacino), frisked when he enters an Italian restaurant, finds a gun his associates had stashed above the toilet in the restroom. He returns to the table to assassinate a crooked police captain.

●

FUN WITH DICK AND JANE (1977)
Suburbanites Dick and Jane Harper (George Segal and Jane Fonda) covertly plot their future life in crime while Fonda pees.

●

SIXTEEN CANDLES (1984)
The Geek (Anthony Michael Hall) charges the school's nerds admission to the boys' restroom for an exhibition of Samantha's (Molly Ringwald) panties.

●

STRIPES (1981)
John Winger (Bill Murray) faces off with the wily Sergeant Hulka (Warren Oates) in a one-punch fight that leaves Winger gasping for air on the latrine floor.

●

WITNESS (1985)
While using a stall in a Philadelphia train-station bathroom, a young Amish boy (Lukas Haas) witnesses the murder of an undercover police officer. The terrified boy sets the film's plot in motion.

●

CROCODILE DUNDEE (1986)
Mick Dundee (Paul Hogan) delights in the Plaza Hotel's "indoor dunny," washing his socks in the bathtub and his feet in the bidet.

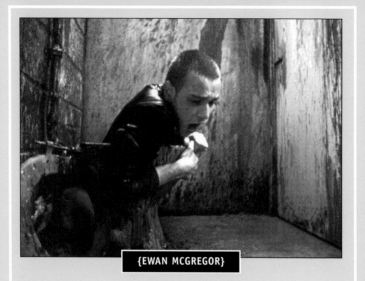

{EWAN MCGREGOR}

TRAINSPOTTING (1996)
In a jarring sequence, junkie Rent Boy (Ewan McGregor) is swallowed whole by the filthiest toilet ever seen.

•

THERE'S SOMETHING ABOUT MARY (1998)
Ted Stroehmann (Ben Stiller) has an unfortunate encounter with the zipper of his tuxedo before going to his high school prom.

•

CATCH ME IF YOU CAN (2002)
While aboard an airplane, the legendary con artist Frank Abagnale Jr. (Leonardo DiCaprio) manages to escape FBI agent Carl Hanratty (Tom Hanks) by dismantling the airplane's bathroom—and climbing out through the toilet system.

Though indoor toilets were fairly common in urban settings by the early part of the century, the *Encyclopaedia Britannica* did not include "plumbing" in its listings until 1911, at which time the trade was described as "work done for the purpose of fitting up and maintaining water service, gas service, and drainage in a building."

....

Alka-Seltzer fizzes because citric acid reacts with sodium bicarbonate when placed into the activating medium of a glass of water. The "plop, plop, fizz, fizz" jingle was composed in 1976 by Tom Dawes:
"Plop, plop, fizz, fizz. Oh, what a relief it is."

•

Some other prominent bathroom-related jingles:
*"You'll wonder where the yellow went
When you brush your teeth with Pepsodent."*—1946

•

"Brylcreem, a little dab'll do ya."—1953

....

94% of Americans say they brush nightly

81% say they do it first thing in the morning

Obviously, some of them are doubling up.

BATHROOM SIZES
(DEFINED)

Half bath (powder room): Toilet and sink only

Three-quarter bath: Toilet, sink, and shower

Guest bathroom: Usually three quarters, adjacent to a guest bedroom

Child's bathroom: Toilet (can be special kid-sized $10^1/_2$-inch [27 cm] rim height), tub with kid-friendly handles, preset temperature controls for safety, electronic faucets to turn the water off if left running (to avoid flooding and high water bills!)

Full bath: Sink, toilet, tub with shower, perhaps some storage space

Master bath: Single or double sink, often with vanity, large tub, separate shower, ample storage, toilet often in smaller area with own door, makeup table with mirror, etc.

....

ASPARAGUS EXPLAINED!

Asparagus contains sulfurous amino acids, which break down into sulfur-rich compounds on digestion. Methyl mercaptan, the same sulfur group that makes skunks so smelly, causes urine produced after eating asparagus to have a distinctive smell. People long assumed that some unfortunate families carried the stinky-asparagus gene while others came off smelling like a rose. Now it is generally believed that we all urinate methyl mercaptan after eating asparagus, but only some of us are genetically wired to detect the ensuing smell.

WHERE IS THE BATHROOM?

Afrikaans: Waar is die toilet?

Arabic: Ain Alhamaam?

Armenian: Our eh pagh-nikeh?

Basque: Non dago komuna?

Bengali: Gosolkhana kothay, dyakhaben ki?

Bosnian: Gdje je toalet?

Breton: Pelec'h emañ ar privezioù?

Bulgarian: Kade e toaletnata?

Catalan: On és la cambra de bany?

Creole: Ki laplas twalèt-la?

Croatian: Gdje je zahod?

Czech: Kde je záchod?

Danish: Hvor er toilettet?

Dutch: Waar is het toilet?

Esperanto: Kie estas la necesejo?

French: Où sont les toilettes?

German: Wo ist die Toilette?

Greek: Pu' i'ne i tuale'ta?

Hawaiian: Aia I hea ka lua?

Hebrew: Eifo ha'sherutim?

Hindi: Aapkaa snanghar kahan hai?

Hungarian: Hol a mosdó?

Indonesian: Kamar kecil di mana?

Irish: Cá bfhuil seomra na mban (f)/bfhear (m)?

Italian: Dove è il bagno?

Japanese: Toire wa doko desu ka?

Korean: Hwa-jang-sil-i O-die Isum-ni-ka?

Latin: Ubi sunt loca secreta?

Mandarin: Xi shou jian zai na li?

Norwegian: Hvor er toalettet?

Polish: Gdzie jest toaleta?

Portuguese: Onde é o quarto de banho? Onde é o casa de banho?

Romanian: Unde este toaleta?

Russian: Gde zdes tualet?

Spanish: ¿Dónde está el baño?

Swahili: Choo kiko wapi?

Swedish: Var ar toaletten?

Tagalog: Nasaan ang kasilyas?

Thai: Hong-nam-you-tee-nai?

Turkish: Tuvalet nerede?

Ukrainian: De tut tualyet?

Vietnamese: Nhà vê sinh o dâu?

Welsh: Ble mae'r toiled?

Xhosa: Iphi indlu yangasese?

Yiddish: Vu iz der bodtsimer?

Zulu: Likuphi itholethe?

In 2003, a new brand of toothpaste named for two of teendom's toothiest stars made its debut. Mary-Kate and Ashley, the toothpaste, is the product of the Olsen twins' collaboration with Aquafresh on a toothpaste that would appeal to teenagers. The flavor: bubblegum with a hint of mint.

....

THE KING OF TOILET PAPER

Pete Correll is the chief executive officer of Georgia-Pacific, a major manufacturer of many types of paper, not least of which is T.P. He is unofficially called the King of Toilet Paper. "Toilet paper is a wonderful product," he told the *New York Times* in 2004. "Ninety-eight percent of the American public uses it. We don't have research on [the other two percent]."

....

Urinal cakes, usually pink, are placed in public urinals to help control odors. They are made mostly of paradichlorobenzene, which is poisonous if eaten. So don't.

....

THE MAGIC KINGDOM

As the grand opening of Disneyland approached in 1954, Walt Disney Productions was faced with a plumbers' strike. With too few workers to produce adequate bathrooms and drinking fountains, park officials had to choose between them. Not surprisingly, they opted for bathrooms. On the big day, Disney was accused of intentionally trying to jack up sales of soft drinks. Walt's reply: "People can buy Pepsi-Cola, but they can't pee in the street."

BEFORE THE INVENTION OF RELIABLE COMMERCIAL
TOILET PAPER
(FIRST SUCCESSFULLY MARKETED BY THE SCOTT PAPER COMPANY IN 1890), **PEOPLE USED:**

- **Salt-water soaked sponge on a stick** (offered in public restrooms in ancient Rome)
- **Discarded sheep's wool** (used in England during the Viking Age)
- **Scraper** (stick kept in a container by the privy in the Middle Ages)
- **Lace** (used by eighteenth century French royalty)
- **Newsprint, paper catalog pages** (used in nineteenth century America)
- **Snow and tundra moss** (used by early Eskimos)
- **Coconut shells** (used in early Hawaii)
- **Frayed end of an old anchor cable** (used by nineteenth century sailing crews from Spain and Portugal)
- **Corn cobs** (various cultures)
- **Mussel shells** (various seaside cultures)
- **Water and one's left hand** (used in precolonial India)
- **Pages from a book** (various cultures)
- **Balls of hay** (various cultures)
- **Hemp** (various cultures)

The city of Nanaimo, British Columbia, claims to be home to the world's largest bathtub. Measuring more than 30 feet (9 m) long and standing 12 feet (3.6 m) high, it can hold more than 30,000 gallons (110,000 l) of water when filled. (The city is also the site of the annual International World Bathtub Race.)

In 1912, the Mellon Pottery Company of Trenton, New Jersey, made what was then deemed the world's largest tub, for 350-pound (159 kg) President William Howard Taft. A replica of the tub, which could fit four men easily, can be seen (but not bathed in) at the Taft Summer White House in Beverly, Massachusetts.

HOW TO MAKE GIN IN A BATHTUB

Clean the tub thoroughly and plug the drain. Drop in a few handfuls of juniper berries and whatever other spices float your boat (or your ducky). Fill the tub with "neutral spirits" (such as a grain-based distillation). Let steep over a period of days; taste periodically; decant when to your taste.

In a Christmas tradition that dates back to the eighteenth century, citizens in the Catalonia region of Spain form small sculptures of characters defecating, hide them in Nativity scenes, and invite friends over to find them. The figurines are called *caganers*. The traditional *caganer* resembles a red-capped Catalonian peasant, but since the 1940s, some have been crafted to represent specific people, from the Pope to Osama bin Laden. According to Marti Torrent, founder of the Association of Friends of the Caganer, the tradition symbolizes the "fertilization of the earth."

VARIOUS NAMES FOR THE BATHROOM, ESPECIALLY AS RELATED TO THE PLACE OF THE ACTUAL TOILET ITSELF

- **House of Honor** (ancient Israelites)
- **House of the Morning** (ancient Egyptians)
- **Garderobe** (medieval England)
- **Necessarium** (Latin phrase brought into English)
- **Reredorter** (literally, "the room at the back of the dormitory")
- **Privy** (British, current)
- **Jakes** (British, current)
- **Pot** (American, sometimes plural)
- **Bogs** (British)
- **John** (British)
- **Loo** (British, perhaps from the French)
- **Head** (shipboard)
- **W.C.** (British for "water closet")
- **Room 100** (in Europe)
- **Lavatory** (British)
- **Closet or Seat of Ease** (British)

....

SOME FACTS ABOUT DENTAL FLOSS:

- Mass-produced commercial dental floss was first made in 1882, out of silk.
- Dental floss today is most often made of synthetic materials (nylon, even Gore-Tex).
- Dentists recommend that each person buy at least 122 yards (111 m) of floss per year, figuring on using about 1 foot (30 cm) per day.
- In 1994, an inmate at a West Virginia prison made a long braid out of dental floss and used it to scale a wall and escape.

You're playing in the NFL at the Denver Broncos' Invesco Field, and, well, all that Gatorade doesn't come out in sweat. You've gotta go. If you're the home team, you're in luck—just behind the home-team bench, under the stands, is a single-stall toilet for Broncos' players and team personnel only. If you're the visitor, run: You have to go all the way back to your own locker room, about 50 yards (46 m) distant. A real home-team advantage.

TOP ★10★

SHAMPOO
BRANDS IN THE U.S.

1. Pantene	7. Finesse
2. Head & Shoulders	8. Neutrogena
3. Suave	9. Johnson & Johnson
4. Pert Plus	10. Salon Selectives
5. Clairol	
6. L'Oreal	

A loofah may feel like a sponge, but it is not a sea creature. The loofah is an edible gourd of the Old World tropics. There are several species, most of which grow to about 1 foot (30 cm) long. The mature fruits contain a soft, yet coarse, spongy material that, when dried out, makes a fine back scrubber. Before World War II, most loofahs in the U.S. were used as filters in the boilers of ships.

TIPS FOR PERFORMING THE PERFECT SHAVE

1 Shave after showering.

2 Apply a hot, moist towel to a clean face (fig. A). Optional: Apply a pre-shave oil product evenly over the face.

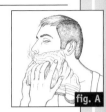

fig. A

3 Apply a thin layer of shaving cream; experts suggest using a badger-hair brush to distribute it (fig. B).

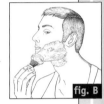

fig. B

4 Using a double or triple blade, begin shaving at the sideburns, working down the face (fig. C). Shave with the grain, or in the direction your hair grows (this usually means shaving down rather than up).

5 Rinse the blades often.

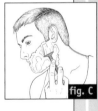

fig. C

6 Shave the neck area using upward strokes (fig. D).

7 Shave the chin and upper lip last to allow shaving cream the most time to soak in and soften the beard.

fig. D

8 When finished, wash your face, and, if desired, apply a small amount of aftershave.

Note: Take your time; a good shave might take ten minutes.

According to **toiletpaperworld.com,** the world's first mass-manufactured toilet paper was made in China in 1391. The Bureau of Imperial Supplies produced 720,000 sheets of toilet paper a year, each sheet measuring 2 feet by 3 feet (0.6 x 0.9 m), for use only by the emperors of China.

| THE AVERAGE PERSON SPENDS ABOUT **3 YEARS** OF HIS OR HER LIFE USING THE TOILET. | THE AVERAGE PERSON VISITS THE TOILET **2,500** TIMES PER YEAR, ABOUT 6 TO 8 TIMES PER DAY. |

The standard procedure for cleaning a portable toilet begins by feeding a hose into the toilet's tank (which can hold from 30 to 50 gallons [113–190 l]) and pumping the contents into a special truck. Seven gallons (26 l) of water mixed with a deodorizing chemical are then poured into the empty tank, the seat area and urinal are wiped down with a towel, and the floor is swept. Finally, a fresh urinal cake is added if the portable potty has a urinal, and the toilet paper is replenished.

IT'S GOOD TO BE KING!
The first year that King Gillette started selling his safety razor—1903—sales totaled 51 razors and 168 blades. By the end of the next year, he had sold more than 90,000 razors and 123,000 blades.

- **Unbleached:** Recycled papers that have not been rebleached.
- **Processed chlorine-free:** Recycled papers bleached with oxygen, ozone, or hydrogen peroxide instead of chlorine chemicals.
- **Totally chlorine-free:** Nonrecycled papers bleached with oxygen, ozone, or hydrogen peroxide instead of chlorine chemicals.
- **Elemental chlorine-free:** Papers bleached with chlorine dioxide instead of chlorine gas. These chemicals still contain chlorine, so toiletpaperworld.com notes the process still produces cancer-causing dioxins. (Note: This accounts for about 60 percent of world market share.)

....

Hemp can be used to make toilet paper. The U.S. Department of Agriculture estimates that one acre of hemp can produce four times more paper than one acre of trees. However, though it is actually legal to grow hemp, a license to cultivate and harvest hemp has never been approved by the USDA.

....

MORE THAN JUST CHEESE

Green Bay, Wisconsin, home to several paper mills, has among its unofficial nicknames "Toilet Paper Capital of the World."

In 2004, inmates at Solano County, California, jails complained that they were not getting enough toilet paper. Officials countered that the inmates were using the paper for much more than its intended function, including molding wet T.P. into sculptures. "I've even seen a toilet paper model of Abraham Lincoln sitting in a chair," one guard told SFGate.com. With average American use at about 57 sheets per day, inmates were using more than 200 sheets daily.

 Home-water-purifiers-and-filters.com claims that people absorb more chlorine by taking a shower than by drinking two quarts (1.9 l) of water.

According to Cromwell and Cruthers, a Canadian skin-products company, one in six men younger than 30 now shaves his genital region.

A 1995 study by Princeton University found that its students' average shower time was **12.5 MINUTES.**

. . . AND A JOY FOREVER

New York's Metropolitan Museum of Art opened an exhibit in 1929 dedicated to the artistic qualities of the bath. A curator said, "The American bathroom is a thing of beauty."

DESIGNER CANS

Jack Nicholson and other celebrities own toilet seats decorated by Sausalito, California, artist Wendy Gold. She uses decoupage to apply artwork to the seats and then seals the creation with varnish. The *Los Angeles Times* reports that Nicholson's seat, a gift from Sean Penn, features vintage postcard pinup girls posing with Nicholson (courtesy of Gold's skill with Photoshop).

GOING ON THE RAILS

On some Amtrak trains, don't bother looking for a handle on the toilet or a button in the wall to flush. Instead, simply close the lid, which will automatically discharge the waste and clean the bowl with a deodorizing solution. A red light glows during this process; when it goes out, the toilet is ready for the next user.

PGBrands.com lists seven Comet-brand products that provide "hospital-grade" bathroom cleaning.

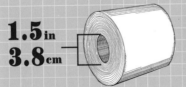

1.5in
3.8cm

Most toilet paper cardboard rolls are 1.5 inches (3.8 cm) in diameter.

WHAT A RACKET!

Flush noise is caused both by the velocity of water flow-ing into the bowl and by water refilling the tank. Quiet toilets rely on gravity to fill the bowl with water. The quietest toilets are one-piece units that flush without a large "head" pressure. (Head pressure is caused by water falling a long distance; water falling, or rather landing, makes a lot of noise.) Typically, the loudest toilets are those that use pressurized flush valves or tanks.

....

By law, all shower heads sold in the United States may deliver a maximum of 2.5 gallons (9.5 l) per minute. At this rate, it takes 24 seconds to fill a gallon jug and 13 seconds to fill a 2-liter bottle. The Federal Energy Management Program estimates an average shower length of 10 minutes or 25 gallons (95 l).

....

A DUBIOUS DEBUT
A rampant Internet rumor says that the first toilet ever seen on television appeared on *Leave It to Beaver* in 1957. The episode (involving a mail-order baby alligator) showed the toilet tank only.

....

Bathtub/shower combinations were first widely avail-able for affordable home use in the late 1960s, thanks in part to emerging plastics and fiberglass technology.

- Pacifiers
- Goldfish
- False teeth
- Socks
- Hamsters
- Mice
- Toy cars
- Rubber ducks
- Action figures
- Barbie dolls
- Underwear
- Bras
- T-shirts
- Shoes
- Toothbrushes
- Jewelry
- Diapers
- Entire rolls of toilet paper

The British Toilet Association holds a national competition called "Loo of the Year." Approximately 400 businesses, historical sites, museums, restaurants, train stations, and other places apply each year and are judged by the association. Anyone can nominate a loo for consideration. Judges award points in categories such as décor and maintenance, fixtures and fittings, cleanliness, equipment, air quality, and accessibility. The awards have been given in 18 categories since 1987.

The Galactika toilet seat is made of clear plastic embedded with LED lights that glow; it is available with five different-colored lights.

IS THAT A ROLL OF TOILET PAPER IN YOUR POCKET?

Johnny Carson is credited with creating a shortage of toilet paper as a result of his opening monologue one night in 1973. Discussing the many shortages of the day (remember the oil crisis, kids?), Carson joked that "stores are even running out of toilet paper." He cited a congressman's statement decrying the lack of government funds for even basic necessities. This was of course a Carsonian exaggeration, but millions took him seriously: After consumers made a mad run on the stuff at stores, Carson and paper executives had to go on the air to say that everything was fine.

This quote about the rise of highly luxurious, ultra-fancy bathrooms, courtesy of a March 2002 *Los Angeles Magazine* article, seems to sum up the phenomenon the best: "They appeared first in Los Angeles, arguably the one place in the nation with the requisite qualities to support them: scores of rich people, houses large enough to incorporate the [fancy bathrooms], and an unusual number of adults who looked good naked."

MERCI, AMBROISE

Kids with cuts and soldiers in the field can thank French doctor Ambroise Paré for convincing the world in the sixteenth century that bandaging wounds was more effective as a cure than cauterizing or reopening them (which until then had been used to cause "laudable pus" to form on the wound).

Mirror: 40 inches (1 m) from the floor to the mirror; up to 48 inches (1.2 m) if the mirror tilts from the wall

Shower Head: 72 to 78 inches (1.8–1.9 m) high, depending on the height of the primary users

Shower: 34 square inches (219 sq. cm) minimum; 30-inch (76 cm) clearance outside the shower

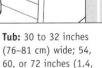

Tub: 30 to 32 inches (76–81 cm) wide; 54, 60, or 72 inches (1.4, 1.5, or 1.8 m) long

Sink: 30 to 32 inches (76–81 cm) high (can be customized for taller or shorter people); 30-inch (76 cm) minimum clearance in front of the sink

Toilet: Rim height of 15 inches (38 cm)—17-inch (43 cm) heights are also available; 48 square inches (309 sq. cm) for clearance, including the toilet fixture

A (BATH)ROOM OF ONE'S OWN

The Palace Hotel in San Francisco was among the first in the country to offer individual toilets for each room. British engineer George Jennings supplied 550 "patent valve closets and traps" in 1878.

....

A homeowner in Del Ray, Florida, installed a special LCD screen behind his bathroom mirror. When turned off, the monitor is invisible; turned on, it plays TV through the mirror. The same bathroom boasts a wireless stereo complete with 50 gigabytes of prerecorded music.

....

Q While taking a shower, sometimes the water temperature changes. Why does that happen, and how can I prevent it?

A This generally happens when people use water from the same water system at the same time (e.g., when flushing a toilet or using the kitchen faucet). This results in lower pressure in the water line feeding your shower faucet. When you have changes in pressure caused by multiple uses on one side and not the other, you will feel the result of different volumes of hot versus cold water. To solve this problem, you can either increase your water piping sizes (which reduces pressure fluctuations) or install a pressure balance device on the hot and cold water that feeds the shower faucet.

TOO HOT TO HANDLE

- Hot water scalds account for 20 percent of all burns in the United States.
- More than 2,000 American children are treated for scalds each year.
- Scalding accidents occur most frequently in the bathroom and kitchen, where they are most preventable.
- Scalding can lead to additional injuries such as heart attacks, shock, falls, and serious broken bones, particularly among the elderly.

Brad Pitt has a bathtub carved from a single piece of limestone, the same stone that forms the 3-inch (7.5 cm) thick walls of the bathroom itself.

Alka-Seltzer was first sold in the United States in 1931. In 1933, it became a staple of the American household, thanks to its reputation as a hangover cure.

"¿DÓNDE ESTÁ B.O.?"

This phrase referring to body odor by its initials first appeared in advertisements for an early antiperspirant product called Odo-Ro-No in 1919. The first commercially available antiperspirant was called Everdry and made its appearance in 1902.

SAY "ACETYLSALICYLIC" THREE TIMES FAST

"Aspirin" is not a generic headache drug; it is the trade name first used by the Bayer Company for the drug acetyl-salicylic acid, which was sold with this name in 1899. The substance was synthesized by Felix Hoffman, a German scientist seeking something that would ease the pain of his father's rheumatism.

The makers of the original Jacuzzi now produce La Scala, a combination home theater and whirlpool bath. Along with the tub, there is a 43-inch (1 m) high-definition TV, a DVD player, stereo, and surround sound. Of course, the remote control floats.

King Tut may have used an acne cream that contained ostrich eggs and bull's urine, along with milk and sea salt.

NAKED CAME THE PRESIDENT

The story goes that President John Quincy Adams chose not to use predecessor President James Monroe's white tub for bathing during his tenure in the White House (1825–1829). He felt that swimming (fully clothed for an additional workout) in the nearby Potomac would serve instead. On one occasion, a small chase boat carrying a servant and dry clothes for Adams sank. Adams gave his wet clothes to his dripping-wet servant and waited naked on the riverbank while the servant returned to the presidential mansion for dry clothing.

Several professional sports leagues (including the National Basketball Association, Major League Baseball, and others) have licensed "celebriducks," rubber duck toys with the billed faces of top players.

STUCK ON YOU

Adhesive bandages became standard bathroom issue not long after their invention in 1921 by Earle Dickson of the Johnson & Johnson Company. His first prototype (allegedly designed to help his kitchen disaster-prone wife) was $2^1/_2$ inches (6.4 cm) wide but 18 inches (45 cm) long, with gauze on one side framed by strips of adhesive glue. It was designed for her to trim to fit her cuts. J&J standardized the $^3/_4$-by-3-inch (1.9 x 7.6 cm) size in 1924.

"Aromatherapy" (the use of smells to treat ailments) was coined in 1928 by French chemist Henri Gattefosse.

Some bathroom scales can measure your percentage of body fat by sending a weak electrical signal right through you. The relative speed of the signal's return through muscle (faster) or fat (slower) is factored in with your height and weight. The result is a body fat percentage.

VARIOUS NAMES FOR
DIFFERENT TYPES —OF COMMON—
BATHROOM TILE

Textured

Smooth

Glazed

Unglazed (must be sealed for protection)

Vitreous glass (sturdy glass that contains colors or patterns)

Terracotta

Mirror

Metallic

Mosaic

Relief (ceramic tiles with a raised pattern beneath the glaze)

Pictorial and patterned

Quarry (floors and hearths)

Pavers (generally for out-side patios and floors, might be used as flooring in outdoor showers)

Marble

Granite

In 1880, the Kampfe brothers patented a safety razor that uses only one side of a two-edged blade. The device included a skin guard made of wire along one side.

GOD IS MY SHOWER

In the 1500s, an ongoing debate raged about the role of bathing in the life of a truly pious Christian. Since the naked body in any form was seen by the Church as "sinful," bathing was frowned upon. Several groups of Protestants and Catholics in France and Germany worked hard to prove that their version of bathwater-free (and thus nudity-free) life was more pious than the other groups'. This followed several centuries of bath avoidance by Christians of all types.

BREATH SAVERS

Why are mints often offered at dinner or found in fine restaurant bathrooms? Peppermint helps one burp, which correspondingly reduces flatulence. It also helps keep your breath minty fresh. On the downside, peppermint can also stimulate stomach acids, thereby causing heartburn.

In the fifteenth century, Aztecs cleansed themselves in steam baths, using natural hot springs or water heated over fires.

COMMON CURRENT BATHTUB MATERIALS

- Cast iron
- Steel
- Acrylic
- Fiberglass

The word *bidet* is from the French word for pony. Why a pony? The use of the device somewhat mirrors an equestrian posture—albeit smaller than a horse. Other foreign terms translate it as "the hygienic little horse" (Italian) and "the guitar" (Spanish).

A company in Japan sells a portable bidet small enough to be carried in a purse.

- **The Power Catalytic Deodorizer**, which automatically dispenses air freshener when the user stands up.
- **Sensors** in the bowl that determine whether the waste is solid or liquid and automatically generate either a light or full flush.
- **The Cyclone Flush**, in either liquid or solid mode, which employs "rim-scouring cyclonic motion," "siphonic jet action," and "rim-scouring power."
- **The Neorest** can include a bidet-like device called a Washletfunction, which uses a warm-water spray to help clean, followed by a warm-air dryer.

....

In the eighteenth and nineteenth centuries, Paris water-sellers traveled the city carrying bathtubs in carts. They would bring the tubs and hot water to customers' homes and apartments.

....

National Bathroom Reading Week is the first full week of June each year in the United States.

....

CLEAN AS A WINDMILL

The phrase "spick-and-span" comes in part from a Dutch word used to describe a ship. In the 1800s, *spiksplinternieuw* became the familiar English phrase, which was first used on the popular cleaning product in 1933.

According to the book *Bathroom Stuff*, every civilization in the world came up with the idea of a comb, except Britons, who had to wait until the Danes showed up in A.D. 789.

The original scent now known as "cologne" is from Germany, not France, via an Italian named Gian Paolo Feminis, who began selling the concoction in 1709 in Cologne, Germany. Feminis sold the stuff as both a topical fragrance and a medicine to be imbibed. French soldiers in Cologne brought cologne back to France to wild acclaim, and Feminis spent the rest of his life fighting off unlicensed competitors. Cologne today comes in a myriad of scents.

PERFUME CHART	
Fragrance Name	Percentage of Perfume Oil
Eau de cologne	3–5
Eau de toilette	5–12
Eau de parfum	12–18
"True" perfume	18 and higher

Microbiologist Charles Gerba conducted a study that showed that Americans use far more toilet paper (an average of seven sheets per visit) than inhabitants of any other country.

SOME PARTS OF THE DWV
(DRAIN, WASTE, AND VENT) SYSTEM

Fixture drain and trap: These small pipes carry water directly out of sinks and showers to waste pipes. The trap is the U-shaped part of the drainage pipe, which holds water and prevents gases from returning through the drain.

Waste pipe: The second-largest pipe in the system, it carries waste from the fixture drains.

Soil stack: The largest pipe in the system, it collects not only wastewater from the waste pipes but waste from the toilet, mixing it all together before emptying it outside the home into the sewer system.

Vents: Air has to enter the drainage system to create smooth water flow in and out. Vents rise to the roofline at several points of the system, usually one per bathroom.

....

Carye Bye, who collected hundreds of postcards featuring bathtubs, created the Bathtub Art Museum online (www.bathtubmuseum.org), which now features occasional "exhibits" of the bathtub in art, photography, and sculpture.

....

Until the advent of plastics in the 1930s, tortoise shell was the most well-known comb material. Other substances used in combs were bone, wood, ivory, celluloid, and various metals.

The word "toilet" is of French origin, from the word *toilette,* meaning the act of washing, dressing, and preparing.

RISQUÉ BUSINESS?

In 1955, ad woman Shirley Polykoff wrote the famous "Does she or doesn't she?" ad campaign for the new Clairol hair-coloring product. *Life* magazine initially refused to run the piece due to its suggestiveness. Clairol, in protest, asked the ad be tested on groups of male and female readers. Every man saw the sexual reference to the woman's, um, agreeability, while none of the women did. The ad was successful: Clairol's sales increased by more than 400 percent over the next 6 years.

The Q in Q-Tips stands for "quality."

Q-Tips were first sold as Baby Gays by Polish-born inventor Leo Gerstenzang in 1925. In 1958, Q-Tips began using the paper sticks that make the product biodegradable when composted.

During World War II, a shortage of lead and tin—previously used to line toothpaste containers—led to the use of laminated toothpaste tubes that used a combination of aluminum, paper, or plastic.

Dental floss was first brought to market by a dentist named Levi Spear Parmly in 1819. Parmly brought his revolutionary waxed silk thread product to England, France, and Canada, as well as his native United States.

....

> Enough dental floss is purchased in America to supply each person with 18 yards (16 meters) per year. To comply with dentists' recommendations to floss with 12 to 18 inches (30–46 cm) each day, that per-person annual total would need to be 120 to 180 yards (110–165 m).

....

T he shortages of World War II meant that silk was no longer available for making dental floss. Mississippi dentist Charles C. Bass created a nylon version, unwaxed and formed from 170 filaments, that he sold wholesale only to dentists who agreed to teach his "Bass Method" of tooth care. He advocated brushing at a 45-degree angle, focusing on the place at which the teeth meet the gums. Then one should floss carefully between all teeth, forming a U-shape with the floss to reach around the larger teeth at the back of the mouth.

....

Johnson's Baby Powder was 70 years old before it was first put into its now-familiar tall, white plastic container in the 1950s. Prior to that, it came in a square aluminum can.

STANDARD TOWEL NAMES AND SIZES
(SIZES MIGHT VARY SLIGHTLY FROM MANUFACTURER TO MANUFACTURER AND FROM COUNTRY TO COUNTRY)

Type	American (inches/centimeters)	European (inches/centimeters)
Washcloth	13 x 13/33 x 33	12 x 12/30 x 30
Guest (or tip)	12 x 18/30 x 46	15 x 26/38 x 66
Hand	16 x 30/41 x 76	20 x 40/51 x 102
Bath	27 x 54/69 x 137	40 x 60/102 x 152
Sheet*	35 x 60/89 x 152	55 x 80/140 x 203
Shower mat	22 x 34/56 x 86	24 x 35/61 x 89

*Sometimes called "jumbo"

A sians tend to have fewer or no apocrine glands, which help produce underarm smells. In Japan, one study showed that 90 percent of the population has no underarm smell at all.

AMERICANS BRUSH THEIR TEETH NEARLY

200

BILLION TIMES A YEAR

AND SPEND MORE THAN

$1.6

BILLION ON TOOTHPASTE.

TWO IN ONE!

Superabsorbent diapers are made with sodium polyacrylate, which is also used to create a gel sprayed on homes to protect them from oncoming fires.

REJECTED NAMES FOR PAMPERS	Dri-Wees	Tads
	Larks	Winks
	Solos	Zephyrs

Marion Donovan entered the trivia books in 1950 by inventing the first practical disposable diaper, called the Boater.

Comedian Jerry Seinfeld on airplane toilets: "I love those small airplane bathrooms. It's like your own little apartment on the plane. You go in, you close the door, the light comes right on. It's a little surprise party every time you go in."

Inspired by military rifles, Jacob Schick invented the magazine repeating razor in 1921: A new blade was revealed as each old blade was discarded, with the new blades being contained in the handle.

THE AVERAGE BABY IS CHANGED
10,000 TIMES
BEFORE IT LEARNS TO USE THE TOILET HIM- OR HERSELF.

Al Moen developed the single-handled faucet in the 1940s.

NECESSITY IS THE MOTHER OF INVENTION
Jacob Schick invented the electric razor after being forced to shave with frigid water while living in Alaska. His first model (1923) was a two-handed job: One hand moved the blades and the other held the large motor. He perfected the one-handed device in 1931 and soon successfully marketed it to a waiting male public.

Alexandre Horowitz, a scientist with the Philips Company of the Netherlands, earned more than 130 patents for shaving-related devices and products in the '30s and '40s.

REASON ENOUGH TO BRUSH

Microorganisms in the mouth feed on leftover food to create acid and particles called volatile sulfur molecules. The acid eats into tooth enamel, producing cavities, while volatile sulfur molecules contribute to bad breath. Fluoride in toothpaste incorporates itself into tooth enamel weakened by acid attack. Some toothpastes contain ingredients that chemically hinder the growth of plaque bacteria. These include ingredients like natural Xylitol and artificial triclosan.

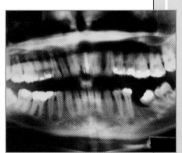

OUCH!

Due to a shortage of razor blades caused by World War II, women on the homefront sometimes resorted to sandpaper to remove leg and underarm hair.

Benjamin Franklin supposedly brought the first bathtub to the United States from France in 1790.

In the late nineteenth century, false eyebrows made from mouse fur were a popular choice for women—a style that persisted until the late 1920s.

THEY GAVE A MOUTHFUL!

Some of the first popular dentures were made in France in the 1820s with "Waterloo teeth"—that is, human teeth taken from the mouths of dead soldiers killed in the Napoleonic Wars. After the American Civil War, teeth from the battlefield dead were shipped to England to make dentures.

The pop-up box that dispenses most facial tissue was invented by Andrew Olsen in 1921.

The popular o.b. brand of tampons derives its name from the German *ohne Binde*, meaning "without napkin."

GOT A TOOTHACHE?
Pray to St. Apollonia, a third-century Christian martyr whose teeth were extracted as torture by Roman soldiers.

The debut of commercially available feminine napkins was delayed by decades due to concerns about advertising the products. In the 1920s, Kotex pads were finally available, thanks to a post–World War I surplus of Cellucotton (the same material used to create Kleenex). However, advertisements for various "feminine" products weren't seen or heard on American airwaves until 1972.

During the 2002 NFL season, police working at Green Bay Packers games in Wisconsin were put on extra alert to combat a growing trend: fans using sinks as urinals to avoid long lines.

....

A FAMILY AFFAIR

The name of the Maybelline cosmetics line comes from company creator T. L. Williams's sister Mabel.

....

Victor Kiam, founder of Remington Products, Inc., became a household name in 1979 when he appeared in a series of commercials touting his purchase of the Sperry Rand shaving company. He claimed in the ads that he "liked the shaver so much, I bought the company!"

....

RELIEF FOR STUFFY NOSES EVERYWHERE!

Kleenex is a brand name, trademarked by the Kimberly-Clark Corporation. Dozens of other companies make a facial tissue of similar style, but "there is only one Kleenex." Kimberly-Clark developed the product in the 1920s while trying to dispose of piles of stuff called "Cellucotton," first made as a wadding for hospitals in World War I.

The name of the fashion products company L'Oreal comes from Auréole, the name French inventor Eugène Schueller gave to the synthetic hair color he created.

The first hair curling irons were heated iron bars used by Assyrians more than **3,500** YEARS AGO.

NO MORE GOING TO BED WITH WET HAIR

Two independently produced electric hair dryers were introduced to an eager public almost simultaneously in 1920 by a pair of Racine, Wisconsin, firms. Racine Universal made the "Race," while Hamilton Beach produced the "Cyclone." Both were all metal and very dangerous to touch when hot.

Dr. Earle Haas of Denver invented a tampon with applicator, which he trademarked as Tampax in the early 1930s. He later sold the rights to the product to Gertrude Tenderich, who formed the Tampax Sales Corporation in 1934.

The first female African-American millionaire made her fortune in hair products. Sarah Breedlove Walker, better known as Madam C. J. Walker, produced various products and hot combs that black consumers used to straighten their hair to conform to the fashions of the early part of the twentieth century.

A SMARTER BATHROOM

Europeans aren't standing still when it comes to bathroom innovation. Philips HomeLab opened in 2004 in the Netherlands to study how people interact with prototypes of intelligent technology in all rooms of the home, including the bathroom. The HomeLab includes a bathroom mirror that integrates data and video displays, providing news, traffic, weather, and voice-controlled TV tuning. HomeLab study participants, says Philips, appreciated the ability to watch the news and traffic while also shaving or brushing their teeth. (Just hope it comes with a defogger as well!) In fact, Philips introduced the Mirror TV in June 2004 as the first commercial product to come out of the HomeLab project. The Mirror TV integrates a 17-, 23-, or 30-inch (43, 58, or 76 cm) LCD using a polarized mirror technology to transfer close to 100 percent of the light through its reflective surface.

....

SUNSETS AND SOAP

In 2003, the Ritz-Carlton, Philadelphia, replaced all its bathroom TVs with 10-inch (25 cm) plasma screens. San Francisco's Mandarin Oriental Hotel has floor-to-ceiling windows in many of its bathrooms, giving bathers a view of the Golden Gate Bridge or Alcatraz while they soak.

....

One cure for women suffering from "suffocating humors of the brain" in Renaissance Italy was to shave their body hair (full body hair growth was the fashion of the day). The idea was to let the "bad humors" flow out of the body more easily.

That little doily thing found on the top of the back of your grandmother's chair is called an antimacassar. It kept the furniture free from a type of hair oil, primarily used by men, called Macassar.

The average American woman uses

11,000
tampons during her lifetime.

AN EXCELLENT INVENTION

In 1906, Hungarian-born inventor Max Kiss used phenolphthalein, a chemical used in winemaking, to create Ex-Lax, the first widely popular laxative. Kiss first tried the name Bo-Bo but settled on shorthand for "excellent laxative." A fig-flavored version proved to be nowhere near as popular as the chocolate-based style.

The inventor of ChapStick, C. D. Fleet, sold his creation to a fellow Virginian named John Morton in 1912 for five dollars. Morton took the sticks nationwide as the first popularly available remedy for chapped lips. Soldiers in World War II received the petroleum and wax mixture in Army-appropriate olive-colored tubes.

Enamel Saver	44
CloSYSII	53
Colgate	68
Tom's of Maine	93
Mentadent	103
Crest	106
Colgate Platinum	106
Aquafresh Whitening	113
AIM	185
Close-Up	218

MIRROR, MIRROR, ON THE WALL . . .

Mirror glass was first created in Venice, Italy, in 1507, by backing transparent glass (first created in 1460) with a sheet of mercury and tin. Glassmakers in the small Italian city-state protected their mirror monopoly for more than a century (in 1664, two Venetian mirror turncoats were murdered to prevent them from revealing the secret), until French spies managed to bring the technology to Paris in the late 1600s.

Lipstick dispensers were transformed from a powder container to the sliding tube style familiar today via the metal case invented by American Maurice Levy in 1915.

Prior to the creation of Nivea in Germany in 1912, with its special formulation of emulsifying water and various oils, skin moisturizers used animal fats as the basic ingredient. In Australia, emu fat remains popular as a skin softener.

....

SHAVE AT YOUR OWN RISK

In European households it is not uncommon for mirrors to be covered with black cloths for a short time following a death in the family.

....

Stylists in ancient Egypt were the first to use two-sided combs with wide and fine rows of teeth.

....

SAME BRAND, DIFFERENT NAMES	
Name	Area
Oil of Olay	North America
Oil of Ulay	England
Oil of Olaz	Europe

....

In the second century, the Greek healer Galen first created a substance similar to today's cold cream by mixing rose petals with melted wax, oil, and water.

....

Ancient Chinese (circa 3000 B.C.), Romans (circa 200 B.C.), and Germans (circa A.D. 400) all used urine for gargling.

Listerine is named for Sir Joseph Lister, a surgeon who was among the first to promote sterile surgery. It was invented by Dr. Joseph Lawrence and was first marketed not as a mouthwash, but as a multipurpose antiseptic. It became popular as a mouthwash in the 1920s.

Why Chanel No. 5? That was Coco Chanel's lucky number. She introduced the revolutionary fragrance to the public on May (the fifth month) 5, 1921.

The red nail polish known as Vamp, popularized by actress Uma Thurman in the 1994 movie *Pulp Fiction*, is the Chanel company's top-selling product of all time.

The first non-clear, colored nail polish was released by Cutex in 1917. It was pink.

TAKE A WHIFF

Sandalwood from India is among the most popular sources for the scents in many perfumes. The process for harvesting sandalwood is extremely labor intensive—but not for people. Sandalwood harvesters first chop down the trees, and then termites are allowed to chew through the outer bark to reveal the inner scented wood.

AVON CALLING

The first Avon Lady was a man, David McConnell, who began working for the company in 1886.

A 1770 British law banned the use of makeup by women attempting to coax gentlemen into their carriages, calling the women witches.

A **"nose"** is a person employed by a perfume company to help create scents. Highly trained noses can sniff out a particular scent amid a mix of more than 100 smells.

DEATH FROM VANITY

Until the late eighteenth century, face powder was lead-based, and rouge contained elements of mercury. The use of such products in the Elizabethan age shortened many lives.

C osmetics company founder Max Factor perfected the brand of foundation he marketed in thin disks under the name "Pan-Cake Makeup" in 1937.

RUB ON A BIT OF LUCK

Rabbits' feet were once used as makeup applicators in early twentieth-century America.

Having a beard in Russia in 1705 was punishable by a fine or jail time, per the decree of Peter the Great.

Fidel Castro's beard owes its longevity to the Cuban leader's revolutionary spirit. He reportedly decided to stop shaving to save more time for leading his people and his movement. He claims it saves him 10 days a year.

Businessman King Camp Gillette and scientist William Nickerson together created the first safety razor in 1903, featuring a single inexpensive disposable steel blade inside a protective metal sleeve.

Sheffield, England, home to a renowned metal works and famous for its steel, was the birthplace, in the early 1700s, of the well-known straight razor.

 The average man spends approximately 140 days of his life engaged in shaving.

Until the early 1900s, definition 8c of the word "toilet" in the Oxford English Dictionary was "preparation for execution by guillotine."

PRIMITIVE PIPING

Clay pipes carried water to buildings in ancient Pakistan (circa 2700 B.C.). In Egypt 300 years later, engineers used copper to form crude water transportation systems.

Today, the degradation of the inner life is symbolized by the fact that the only place sacred from interruption is the private toilet.
—Lewis Mumford

THE
★ 1ST ★
BRECK GIRL

17-year-old Roma Whitney made her debut in 1936. Dr. John Breck promoted his shampoo, first sold in 1930, as the first commercial shampoo in America.

The Hindi word pronounced "champo," meaning "to massage," is the root of the word *shampoo*. The word entered the English language in the seventeenth century, reflecting the practice whereby wealthy Britons in India had their hair massaged with exotic oils. The substances later took on the name of the action.

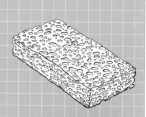

{NATURAL}

{SYNTHETIC}

A sponge is made of the remains of sea animals whose decay has formed "spongin," a substance similar to some types of horns or antlers. Synthetic sponges, created by injecting air into special polymers, were first formed in the 1940s.

The lather created by shampooing does not help clean your hair. Lather is formed by the detergent when it surrounds air instead of the oils on the hair.

WORK UP A SWEAT WHILE YOU SHOWER

Attendees of the 1900 Paris Exhibition saw an early model of a shower in which users rode a bicycle-like gadget to pump the water up to a water tank, from whence it fell back down on them as they rode.

Ancient Greek gymnasiums featured wall-mounted gargoyles whose mouths formed shower head–like openings.

Here are some tips for giving an elephant a shower, according to Absolut Elephant, the pachyderm-centric Web site (www.elephant.se). While its expansive sides are easy to reach and clean, make sure to clean behind the ears, inside of the hind legs, in the pockets where the tusks becomes visible, the wrinkles in front of or under the eye, the temporal gland, the nails and the area above the nails, the stomach, and under the tail. Too often, the back is not regularly cleaned and the supra skin not removed, thus some animals retain layers of dead skin over their back. Make sure to get your brush up there, too.

IVORY SOAP'S OTHER 56/100 %		
Uncombined alkali	0.11
Carbonates	0.28
Mineral water	0.17

The world's most expensive sink is made by Nevobad of Germany. The golden sink encrusted with nearly 500 precious gems sells for about $250,000.

In Asia, women most often use a gel or bar soap and their hands while bathing, while 76 percent of American women use some sort of scrubbing or washing aid, such as a sponge or cloth.

A HANDY CONFIGURATION

The cold water is on the right on standard faucets because most people are right handed. At one time, only a single handle existed on faucets; it was on the right side and was for cold water only.

In most of the Arab world, one should never touch food with the left hand, which is traditionally reserved for use when wiping up after using the toilet.

In 1714, Daniel Fahrenheit, a German resident of Holland, created the first mercury thermometer and with it the scale Americans use today. Twenty-eight years later, Swedish astronomer Anders Celsius created his own scale.

The Porter Thermometer Museum is located in Onset, near Buzzard's Bay, Massachusetts. It houses the 3,800-plus thermometer collection of Richard Porter.

Thanks to British inventor Walter Alcock's ideas in 1879, toilet paper is perforated and put on a roll to allow for the tearing off of various lengths.

THREE ANCIENT TOILETS

Archaeologists have unearthed 5,000-year-old indoor toilet facilities on the Orkney Islands (off Scotland). In the ancient Pakistani city of Mohenjo-daro, sit-down toilets were made in about 2500 B.C.

The first toilet paper sold in the United States, on shelves in the 1850s, was a decided flop. Most people had plentiful (and free) alternatives and didn't see the need to switch to a commercial product. The Scott brand of toilet paper was the first to meet with wide success not long after the company's debut in 1879.

A $66,000 TOILET
A space-age, self-cleaning public toilet debuted at a Metro stop in Virginia in 2003. Along with the ability to clean itself (as well as wash the floor after every 30 uses), the toilet provides piped-in music and no-touch flushing.

WOMEN TAKE 3 TIMES AS LONG AS MEN TO USE THE TOILET.

During Napoleon's reign, a chamber pot popular in England was decorated with the French emperor's face (on the inside, of course).

WHAT PEOPLE WOULD LIKE IN THEIR BATHROOMS AS FANTASY EXTRAS

THE TOP 5 REPLIES:

- Musical toilet-paper holder
- Gold faucet and taps
- Built-in stereo
- A heated seat
- A copy of *Jane's Fighting Ships*

Did we mention this was a British survey?

....

Dr. Sheffield's Crème Dentifrice was created in Connecticut in 1892 as the first toothpaste to be sold in tubes that rolled as they were emptied.

....

From *The Family Instructor of the Knowledge of Medicine*, written in 1760, the recipe for the King of France's tooth powder:

Take of chalk and pebble-stones burnt, of each one oz. Myrrh, bole-armoniac and dragon's-blood, of each half an ounce, of ammoniacum and cuttle-bones, of each 3 drachms, let them be all finely powder'd.

No word on how to get the dragon's blood.

....

Hippocrates, in his recipe for toothpaste, included ground mice, rabbit skulls, and white stone.

THE VALUE OF A PRAYER

In the seventh century, Mohammed wrote that a prayer that was said with a clean mouth (i.e., after using a toothbrush-like device known as a *misswak*) was worth 70 normal prayers.

....

Q Why don't low-flush (1.6 gallon/6 liter) toilets now mandated in any new or remodel construction work as well with older plumbing as with new?

A Older pipes were 4 to 6 inches (10–15 cm) in diameter, while modern pipes are a standard 3-inch (7.6 cm) diameter. This means that there is less water in the wider pipes to move the waste along its path.

....

Former English jailbird William Addis popularized the bristled toothbrush after his release from prison in 1770. After discovering its salutary effects while in the stir, he began to try to sell them as well as promote their use through talks and advertisements.

....

The electric toothbrush made its American debut in 1960. Marketed by Squibb as the Broxodent, it was modeled after a Swiss design.

....

For some hemorrhoid sufferers, use of a squat toilet is recommended. Medical supply companies provide a sort of booster seat that fits around a standard seat to convert it into a squat toilet.

The Smith Brothers of cough drop fame were named William and Andrew.

....

Oral-B toothbrushes were carried on the 1969 Apollo XI mission, the first moon landing.

....

The first toothbrush in space was Eugene Cernan's personal toothbrush, a Lactona that he took with him on Apollo X, which orbited the moon in 1969. The toothbrush and a spoon he also brought along sold at auction for $10,000 in April 2003.

....

PORTABLE POTTIES

French and British royalty and gentry did not have to visit unpleasant privies while traveling. They carried with them a portable privy called a "close stool" (*chaise percée* in French). English writer Samuel Johnson disliked the fancy facilities, claiming that the quilted seats therein "retain a bad smell. There is nothing so good as the plain board."

....

Current U.S. federal law requires that residential toilets manufactured after January 1, 1994, must use no more than 1.6 gallons per flush (6 lpf). Early attempts to meet the standard with low-flush toilets led to clogging and double-flushing, which pretty much defeated the purpose. Newer versions are much more efficient.

The water in colonial America had a distinctly wooden taste; water pipes were usually made from hollow logs.

GOOD BATHROOM CHI

According to feng shui principles, blue towels are the best color towels for a bathroom, where they improve the flow of the water element.

Fluoride in water and toothpaste aids in the prevention of tooth decay by helping minerals reinforce the enamel in teeth.

FROM THE U.S. MARINES MANUAL ON GROOMING FOR FEMALE MARINES

"If worn, nail polish and non-eccentric lipstick will harmonize with the scarlet shade used in various service and dress uniform items (i.e., scarlet cord on green service cap, scarlet trim on blue dress uniform, and scarlet background on enlisted insignia of grade), in shades of red, and may be worn with the service, blue dress, blue-white dress, and evening dress uniforms."

Urine, with its cleansing ammonia, was an ingredient in toothpaste until the eighteenth century.

Plumbers report that powder room toilets clog up more often than ones in master bathrooms because these smaller rooms, with only a toilet and no shower or bathtub (as in half-baths), do not have the added water flow of a bath or shower to empty shared drainpipes.

Terry cloth was first woven in France in 1841.

Vaseline can stay soft and pliable even to 40 degrees Fahrenheit below zero (-40°C).

British scientist R. V. Jones boasted in his book, *Most Secret War*, that he won a contest by urinating over a 6-foot (1.8 m) wall.

A TEASPOON A DAY . . .

Vaseline inventor Robert Chesebrough, who first set up a factory to extract his "petroleum jelly" from crude oil, truly loved the product that made him rich. Not only did he use himself as a guinea pig during testing—cutting or burning his skin to test Vaseline's efficacy at wound protection—he also ate a spoonful of the stuff every day. He died in 1933 at the age of 96.

King James I of Scotland met his end in a privy pit in 1437. After attempting to hide from attackers in the pit, he was discovered and stabbed to death.

★ **MEDIEVAL** ★
NAMES FOR
THE TOILET
ROOM

• Garderobe (clothes closet)	• Place of easement
• Priest's hole	• Oratory
• Privy	• Chapel

MEN'S ONLY
The U.S. Senate chambers did not have a bathroom available for female senators until 1992. Prior to that, the female senators used the same restrooms used by tourists.

In 1183, a large contingent of the leaders and most important knights of Holy Roman Emperor Frederick I's court were drowned when their meeting room floor collapsed and they plunged into the privy cesspool below.

LOOK OUT BELOW
The British term for the toilet, *loo*, may have come from the French expression *gardez-l'eau*, meaning, essentially, "watch out for the water," as waste was tossed from a chamber pot into the street below. Though defenestrating waste was permitted, tossing the entire chamber pot from the window to the street was banned in Paris in 1395.

Many garderobes were built in the exterior upper walls of castles, with their doors facing inward and with their undersides (and a user's underside) exposed to the air. The garderobe's opening also proved a useful, if ill-smelling, entry point for invading soldiers.

....

IT'S IN THE VAULT
Paleoscatology is the study of fossilized excrement. British archaeologists excavating near York, England, in 1972 discovered a 1,200-year-old piece perhaps deposited by a visiting Viking. It is nicknamed "The Lloyds Bank Turd," as it was found on land now occupied by the bank.

....

A toilet on board a boat or ship is referred to as "the head." The term is used in many maritime phrases to mean "top" or "forward." In older sailing ships, the head was the forward part of the ship, where the toilet area opened through to the sea. Thus, the name remains on toilet facilities afloat today.

....

GODS OF EXCREMENT
The ancient Roman god of dung was called Stercutius. The Moabite god of similar stature was called Bel-Phegor. Devotees traditionally left appropriate offerings at Bel-Phegor's shrine.

....

Japanese towels include the *furoshiki*, for putting on the floor to dry the feet, and the *tenugui*, a towel that is wrung out after absorbing water from the user's body.

LENIN IS SPINNING IN RED SQUARE

The 3D-Gold jewelry shop in Hong Kong offers a special treat to any customer who purchases more than $200 of its product: a visit to the store's gold and jewel-encrusted bathroom, built at a cost of more than $3 million. Owner Lam Sai-wing was inspired by a 1921 saying by Lenin, which noted that a solid-gold toilet would be the ultimate example of capitalist waste.

....

Aztecs shaved with razors made of volcanic obsidian rock.

....

To help users locate outhouses in the dark, American homeowners in the nineteenth century often tied a string between the house and the facility. Feeling along the string led to the seat of ease. During the day, the string was handy for hanging clothes to dry.

....

WHY CALL IT THE LOO?

The British term *loo* for the bathroom has many possible etymologies. Some hyothesize its origins in the French expression *gardez l'eau* (see page 60). Or, it may derive from the French word *le lieu* (meaning "place" or "spot"), used to indicate the place of the bath in eighteenth-century architectural drawings. It may also also have come from calling the water closet the "Waterloo." Another theory comes from Italy, where the bathroom was (and in some places is) known as *numero cento* (or "one-hundred") in hotels. Numerically represented by "100," it looks like the word loo.

A DIFFERENT KIND OF OFFERING

French women suffering through long sermons or speeches during the reign of Louis XIV employed portable chamber pots shaped somewhat like a gravy boat. One bathroom history book says that the containers were named *bourdaloues*, after a particularly long-winded parson of the period.

....

The first urinals were built by Roman emperor Vespasian in about A.D. 40. He charged prominent citizens a small fee to use these special facilities, then sold their urine to cloth dyers. According to Suetonius, when his son complained about the smell of the urinals and tanks, the profit-oriented emperor replied, "but the money doesn't smell."

....

FROM A UNITED PRESS INTERNATIONAL REPORT, NOVEMBER 2003

Forty-one-year-old Edwin Gallart of New York City dropped his cell phone into the toilet on a train, and as he tried to retrieve it, his arm got stuck.

Rescue crews had to be called to meet the train to free Gallart, and the commuter line Metro-North considered charging him for part of the railroad's "multiple thousands" of dollars it cost for the rescue, extra train, and rerouting costs.

"We will definitely look into the possibility of any sort of recompense," says Dan Brucker, a spokesman for Metro-North.

"It is standard operating practice for us to do this, given that it is taxpayers' funds that have gone down the drain, so to speak."

When using the incinerator toilet, following use, flip a lever to release waste into a sealed container below the bowl. Then push a button (after getting up, please), and the waste is incinerated. The container of ash can be periodically emptied.

....

BIBLICAL BATHROOM INSTRUCTIONS, FROM DEUTERONOMY 23:12–13

"Thou shalt have a place also without the camp, whither thou shalt go forth abroad. And thou shalt have a paddle upon thy weapon; and it shall be, when thou wilt ease thyself abroad, thou shalt dig therewith, and shalt turn back and cover that which cometh from thee."

....

According to the *Scottish Medical Journal*, three people in Glasgow were treated in 1993 for injuries sustained when their toilets unexpectedly collapsed.

....

SIGNS ON MEN'S AND WOMEN'S ROOMS SEEN BY TRAVELERS

Pointers and Setters	Dir and Mna (Gaelic)
Kings and Queens	Blokes and Sheilas (Australia and Outback Steakhouses)
Buoys and Gulls	
Nam and Nu (Vietnamese)	Mannen and Vrouwen (Dutch)

A 1995 funding crisis caused some office suppliers to refuse to deliver to Washington, D.C., district government offices, depriving workers of toilet paper for several days.

....

IT'S A CRAPPER!

According to a story in *Plumbing and Mechanical* magazine, American World War I soldiers stationed in England brought home the slang term "crapper" for the toilet after seeing so many devices there emblazoned with the corporate name "T. Crapper/Chelsea." The company had been originally founded by Thomas Crapper in 1861. However, the word "crap" for feces is not derived from that Victorian-era plumber's name; most etymologists trace that to an Old Dutch word, *krappe,* or Lower German, *krape*, meaning "a vile and inedible fish."

....

Thomas Crapper, though not the inventor of the flushing toilet, did patent several other toilet devices. Among these was the "disconnecting trap," which helped prevent backflow of waste into the toilet. Crapper's company outfitted various royal palaces with toilet facilities, including Buckingham Palace and Windsor Castle. The Crapper Company later had a "Royal Appointment" to King Edward VII and King George V. Tourists visiting Westminster Abbey find the manhole covers there with the name "Crapper" and make brass rubbings as souvenirs.

Chamber pots were the preferred waste-containment system in Europe for several hundred years. Among the famous names who created cabinets and chairs to hold the pots were Chippendale, Hepplewhite, and Sheraton.

....

Toilet mapping is the practice of locating public facilities before the need for them arises. According to one survey, two thirds of people work hard to know where to go when they need to go. Older people are more often toilet mappers. However, on one episode of *Seinfeld*, George Costanza (Jason Alexander) claimed to be able to locate a public restroom at any location in greater Manhattan.

....

Every now and then, pour a shot of cooking oil into your boat's toilet, especially if it's difficult to pump. This will lubricate the seals, "O" rings, and moving parts, according to the Web site boatsafe.com.

....

DON'T BE SHY

According to the International Paruresis Association, paruresis, also called "bashful bladder syndrome," is a social phobia in which a person fears being scrutinized or criticized by others when urinating in a public restroom. The IPA reports that 7 percent of Americans, or 17 million people, suffer from some level of paruresis, from mild to a total inability to urinate in a public restroom.

HOVERCRAFT

A 2001 survey by a bathroom tissue company found that 60 percent of respondents did not actually sit on public restroom toilet seats but rather hovered slightly above them. The survey also reported that 40 percent used their shoe to flush the public toilet when done, with another 20 percent using a paper towel.

According to surveys

7 out of 10 Americans report closing the bathroom door even when alone at home.

In 1982, the British rock group The Clash inserted part of the 2000 Flushes commercial jingle into its song "Inoculated City." The group was sued by the manufacturer and forced to remove the bit from later versions (though negotiations later allowed other compilations of Clash hits to include the jingle).

LOSER CLEANS THE FLOOR

The *Orlando Sentinel* reported in 2003 that an electronic entertainment company was working on a game to be played at a men's urinal in which the flow (direction and aim) from a person's visit was key to winning.

FAMOUS PEOPLE
WHO DIED IN THE BATHROOM
OR WHILE USING THE FACILITIES

- **Heliogabalus,** emperor of Rome, murdered by his own bodyguards, 222
- **Arius,** Christian theologian, possibly from poison, 336
- **King Edmund II of England,** "stabbed from beneath as he answered a call of nature," 1016
- **King James I of Scotland,** killed by assassins, 1437
- **King Henry III of France,** stabbed by a Jacobin friar, 1589
- **Arthur Capel,** earl of Essex, slit own throat while imprisoned in the Tower of London, 1683
- **King George II of Great Britain,** died in the bathroom after breakfast, 1760
- **French revolutionary Jean-Paul Marat,** stabbed to death while taking a bath in 1793, by Charlotte Corday (a famous wax figure of the scene can be found at Madame Tussaud's Wax Museum in London)
- **Catherine the Great,** empress of Russia, had a fatal stroke on the commode in St. Petersburg, 1796
- **Lenny Bruce,** American comedian, overdosed on heroin, 1966
- **Elvis Presley,** icon, died of natural causes or drug overdose, 1977

....

In 2003, TBS, the U.S. cable channel, put flat-screen TVs in American sports bar men's rooms. As a patron approaches a urinal equipped with such a device, it automatically switches on and plays a video promoting the cable network's sports programming.

Using a shaving brush (as opposed to one's hand) to apply shaving cream "stimulates the arrector pili muscles—the same ones that make the hair on the back of your neck stand up," a barber told the *Los Angeles Times* in 2003.

A shaving brush should be used in a circular clockwise motion, not back and forth like a paintbrush.

Badger hair makes the best shaving brushes. High-end models (such as the Art of Shaving's High Mountain model) can go for more than $400.

BATHROOM HUMOR

To promote the 2003 hit kids' novel *The Day My Butt Went Psycho*, Scholastic placed advertisements in bathrooms in several U.S. family-oriented restaurant chains, including Applebee's, Chi-Chi's, and T.G.I. Friday's. *Zombie Butts from Uranus* is the next book in the series.

As the "metrosexual" craze spread in 2003, barbers and salon owners noted a rise in the sales of badger-hair shaving brushes and other men's high-end grooming devices.

SHAVER WARS

In 2003, Gillette sued Schick, alleging patent infringement because Schick's "Quattro" four-blade razor closely resembled the Gillette three-blade "Mach3" model. In 2004, Schick returned the favor, claiming that Gillette falsely advertised that its products (inferior in Schick's eyes) provided the "world's best shave(s)" as well as for copyright infringement on earlier razor models. Gillette fired another salvo in the shaver wars with the 2004 introduction of the battery-powered M3Power. Tiny pulses from the head of the shaver supposedly make the hairs stand up straighter.

....

In 2002, Gillette's Mach3 shaving systems raked in $2 billion in sales, according to the *New York Times*, making it the best-selling line of razors on the market.

....

Visitors to Samarkand, Uzbekistan, should know that the small clay balls provided in public toilets are to be used as toilet paper.

....

The MSN division of Microsoft is working on developing the iLoo, creating wireless Internet access points at portable toilet facilities. The idea is to place a plasma screen with a waterproof keyboard in a convenient place for visitors. The *Seattle Post-Intelligencer* also reported that the company was talking to toilet-paper makers about imprinting Web addresses on the paper.

{JANET LEIGH}

LOCK YOUR BATHROOM DOOR

According to Alfred Hitchcock, his 1960 film *Psycho* was the first major movie to show bathroom fixtures in a way that furthered the plot. No one was hurt, though—the "blood" that swirls down the shower drain after Marion Crane (Janet Leigh) is killed was made of chocolate syrup.

John and Abigail Adams, the first residents of the White House, relied on servants to lug water five blocks to fulfill their bathroom needs. In 1831, work was begun on a piping system (first wooden, later iron) that brought water from a nearby spring into the residence. It was operational by 1833. In 1853, water heaters began to provide running hot water. By 1876, a 2,000-gallon (7,571 l) tank had been installed in the attic to provide bathing water to presidential families.

....

A 1902 renovation of the White House created the first indoor flushing toilets. A 1948 study called the plumbing in the building, which had been haphazardly added to in past decades, "largely makeshift by modern standards and unsanitary." Today, all piping in the building is of highest quality. Hot and cold water lines are made of red brass, while various waste and vent lines are brass and copper tube. Bathrooms on the residence's second floor are equipped with water drinking fountains. Prior to 1948, bathrooms were all separate from bedrooms. The new guest rooms have attached bathrooms.

The Japanese company Toto sells a $100 Travel Washlet, a portable version of its bottom-squirting toilet model.

....

> The average American home uses **185 gallons (700 l)** of water a day. The average African home goes through **1.8 gallons (6.6 l)**. **Seventy-five percent** of American water use is in the bathroom. In North America, nearly **100 percent** of residents have access to a flushing toilet system; that figure is **92 percent** in Europe. In Africa, it is less than **14 percent**.

....

In Roanoke, Virginia, local charities raise money by building a toilet in someone's yard and then charging for removing it. Neighbors can also pay $10 to have a toilet put in someone's yard; the owner of the new "toilet" (they don't really work) can then pay the charity $5 to have it removed. Permanent "no-toilet" insurance is also available for $20. The toilets are purple and pink; local contractors donate the labor.

....

The bathroom is increasingly being closed off as a private intimate space. People clean and regenerate themselves in the bathroom, while also seeking the private sensual and carnal pleasures of a boudoir.
—Annie Ziliani, of Novale Next, a French marketing agency

RECYCLING GOES A STEP FURTHER

The 2003 reHouse project found Swiss engineers creating a toilet that eliminates flushing. Waste is collected in biodegradable paper bags. These are used to create a kind of compost that can be used as plant fertilizer or biogas that can be used to power a cooking stove. Another dry toilet model is called the Solar Composting Advanced Toilet (or S.C.A.T.). Its inventor, Larry Warnberg, also suggests adding earthworms to increase aeration.

....

The 2003 International Dry Toilet Conference was held in Tampere, Finland. Speakers called for a slow end to flush toilets, which they called an "environmental disaster" and far from the best choice for developing nations as they create sewage systems. Critics, however, call the flush toilet ideal for preventing the spread of disease and "one of the greatest public health advances in the modern era." Some dry toliet proponents also point to water waste, but critics note that flushing accounts for less than 10 percent of worldwide water use, with agriculture's 70 percent accounting for the largest use of water.

....

In Japan, the National Toilet Symposium annually declares a Toilet Day and votes on the year's top toilet models.

....

A woman can experience an increase in bad breath just before her menstrual period. Changes in her body's hormones at this time make her gums more likely to produce bacteria that cause odors.

- Matsushita's model sends a mild electric pulse through the body (via the buttocks) to measure the seatee's body/fat ratio.
- The Inax raises the seat and glows in the dark when it senses the body heat of an approaching person—ideal for late-night visits. The Inax comes complete with the choice of six soundtracks that include chirping birds, rushing water, and a Japanese harp.
- Toto's Wellyou II uses a tiny spoon to collect urine and measure urine sugar levels. The hope is that information like this can be sent via a built-in cell phone to doctors, allowing for remote monitoring of patients.
- Matsushita sells a $3,000 toilet that uses air nozzles—hot and cold—to warm or cool the bathroom as needed when a person enters. The Matsushita toilet is one of many Japanese models that lets users set the amount and temperature of a soft spray of water, used for both washing and massage while seated. More Japanese homes have toilets with interior sprays than have personal computers, according to the *New York Times*.

··

Electronics manufacturer Pioneer markets the Happy Aqua Phone, a waterproof case for cell phones. Speakers allow showerers to avoid missing even a moment of time on the phone. *Wired Magazine* featured the phone in its occasional "Japanese Schoolgirl Watch," which it uses to look toward the future of American fads.

HERE ARE **10 PROMINENT PEOPLE**
WHO SUFFERED FROM CONSTIPATION:

- Thomas Jefferson
- Robespierre
- Napoleon
- William Henry Harrison
- Henry James
- Gandhi
- George Gershwin
- Howard Hughes
- Judy Garland

In a house where there are small children, the bathroom soon takes on the appearance of the Old Curiosity Shop.
—Robert Benchley

MONEY WELL SPENT

Japanese consumers spend more than $100 million annually on medicine designed to eliminate or at least minimize odors created while going to the bathroom.

B erkeley architect Sim Van der Ryn was never a booster of the traditional "flush, treat, and dump" system of wastewater management. In 1996, while pondering the work of future archaeologists as they sift through the remains of ceramic toilet bowls, intricate pipe systems, and holding ponds, he imagined them writing: "By early in the twentieth century, urban earthlings had devised a highly ingenious food production system whereby algae were cultivated in large centralized farms and piped directly into a ceramic food receptacle in each home."

A female urinal was introduced by Japan's Toto company in 1951, but it was discontinued in 1968 because of poor sales.

___ SURPRISINGLY, FOR ALL OF JAPAN'S ___
HIGH-TECH ADVANCES IN TOILETRY,

A LATE 1990S SURVEY FOUND THAT ONLY

30% OF JAPANESE HOMES

WERE CONNECTED TO A SEWAGE SYSTEM.

Some Japanese toilets feature a handheld remote control to raise and lower the seat.

DAILY AFFIRMATIONS

U.S. President Harry Truman's bathtub had a message carved in glass on the backside that read: "In this tub bathes the man whose heart is always clean and serves his people truthfully."

Public toilets in London offer for sale various items such as a comb, tissue, or condom, as well as a toothbrush with a dollop of toothpaste already on it.

- A waterless composting toilet that changes waste to an "odorless nutrient-rich fertilizer suitable for your garden." (Cost may be a factor, though, as the unit runs about six grand.)
- Mold- and mildew-resistant hemp shower curtains.
- Low-flow showers that reduce the typical 6 to 8 gallons per minute (23–30 l/min) to as low as 1.4 gallons per minute (5 l/min).
- Water filters on the showerhead and faucet that reduce chlorine and other minerals in the water.
- 17-watt (58 BTU/hr) bulbs that simulate outside, natural light.

A Penn State University student study found that signs reminding bathroom users to wash their hands increased hand-washing by female users by 36 percent but had no effect on men's washing-up activity.

HIGH-TECH SHOWERING

At Toto's research facility in Japan, volunteers take baths while wearing electrodes on their head so researchers can measure the subjects' physiological responses while bathing.

TAKE THE BEAUTIFUL RESTROOM TOUR

Suwon, South Korea, is home to perhaps the most beautiful and popular public toilets in the world. Spurred by the nation's co-hosting (with Japan) of soccer's World Cup in 2002, the city of one million near Seoul went a little nuts. They spent more than $4 million sprucing up their public facilities, then gave public tours and extensively advertised them on buses. According to the *Los Angeles Times*, one ad combining two local landmarks read: "Enjoy the World Heritage Fortress and Beautiful Restroom Tour."

Each specially designed restroom has its own name and design theme, featuring castles, towers, or mountains. Piped-in music, wall art, and skylights are just some of the added touches. One set of urinals is made of glass, so users can look out onto a beautiful natural scene while doing their business. All the toilets employ the "etiquette bell," which makes a sound like running water when pressed to mask other sounds produced by the bathroom user.

....

In 2000, Los Angeles artist Xenia Zampolli created a unique new way to decorate toilets. Instead of painting hard ceramic bowls or using stickers or other add-ons, Zampolli works directly on the still-wet porcelain, painting patterns and adding gold leaf, computer chips, shapes of clay, and other objects. After signing the piece, she glazes and fires it. Trendy shops (mostly in California) have found a ready market for her one-of-a-kind installations, which can go for up to $3,500 (without the custom-made seat to match). A leopard-print pattern has proven especially popular.

FACINATING BATHROOM
FACTS ABOUT AMERICANS:

- The number of homes in the U.S. without complete indoor plumbing dropped from more than 720,000 in 1990 to just over 670,000 in 2000.
- Alaska has the lowest proportion of homes with indoor plumbing of any state, with 3.83 percent of Alaskan homes lacking such facilities. (Ten years earlier, the percentage had been 12.5.) Outhouses still service these homes. New Mexico has the greatest number of homes without any form of plumbing, but these 14,228 homes account for only 2.2 percent of the state's total number of homes.
- Researchers speculate that the overall rise in the number of homes with plumbing corresponds to the rise in the use of mobile or trailer homes in the South, which have standard built-in bathrooms.

....

The World Toilet Exhibit, a museum on the island of Shikoku, Japan, features a solid gold toilet and solid gold toilet slippers (another unique Japanese addition to the world of the bathroom).

....

A HARSH LESSON

A terrible 1923 earthquake in Yokohama resulted in widespread disease due to the lack of public facilities. Thereafter, flushing toilets and indoor plumbing became more widespread throughout Japan.

GOING IN SPACE

The International Space Station, rotating serenely 235 miles (378 km) or so above Earth, makes use of special facilities and technology.

- Water and waste pipes are made of titanium and wrapped in metal mesh.
- Pumps and fans are used to move water and waste through the system. (Gravity usually does this job on Earth.)
- The system uses purifiers so powerful that urine from the astronauts can be refined and recycled as drinking water.
- Drinking faucets dispatch a preset amount of water into a plastic bag; without the bag, the water would float freely and perhaps damage sensitive components. Astronauts make a small hole in the bag and drink through that.
- The toilet and the user cannot depend on gravity for waste outflow. To prevent dangerous (and embarrassing) accidents, two machines are positioned strategically to suction urine and feces away from the astronaut.

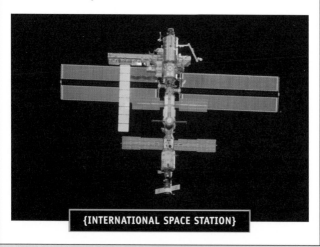

{INTERNATIONAL SPACE STATION}

POLISHING UP OLD AND WEATHERED MARBLE COUNTERTOPS AND SINKS:

1 Wet-sand with 1,000-grit paper (focus only on small scratches; deep ones are there to stay).

2 Rinse and dry the top.

3 Buff using a "medium-cut cleaner" with a small power buffer.

4 Protect the final finish with cultured marble polish.

....

Phnom Penh's annual water festival draws huge crowds to the Cambodian capital. In 2001, residents complained that their yards and alleys were being used as toilets by the visitors, and the city began using portable toilets, mounted on wheels, to help meet the crowds' needs.

....

According to *Sports Illustrated*, locals in Alaska say it can get so cold there that you can "pee and lean on it."

....

North Berwick, Scotland, was home to the 1994 Great Britain Loo of the Year. The $210,000 facility, done in a lovely red and gray Formica, is kept immaculately clean and is supplied with fresh flowers and foliage by two full-time attendants.

MOMENTOUS BATHROOM EVENTS

- Greek war hero **Agamemnon** was killed with an ax by his wife, **Clytemnestra**, while taking a bath.
- **Archimedes** supposedly discovered the physical principle named for him by noticing how the water rose when he entered a bath. The story goes that he leapt out of the bath and ran around naked, shouting "Eureka!" The Archimedean principle states that a body in a liquid is buoyed up by a force equal to the weight of the displaced fluid.
- German composer **Richard Wagner** was well known for his habit of soaking in milk perfume every day while working on his opera *Parsifal*. He also loved to smell the stuff even when not bathing.
- **Edmond Rostand** supposedly created many of his best works, including *Cyrano de Bergerac*, by writing while in the tub, where he could compose without interruptions.
- **George Joseph Smith** murdered three wives over the course of several years, ending in 1914, causing a major scandal in England. Each of the killings took place in a bathroom shortly after he had taken out insurance policies on his victims. He became known as the Bluebeard of the Bath.

A New York City ad agency tested the efficacy of bathroom advertising in the months leading up to the 2000 presidential election. They hung statements about each of the two candidates in toilets. Sixty-two percent of toilet users surveyed remembered the statements; by comparison, only 16 percent of a separate control group remembered an outdoor billboard with a similar message.

TAX DOLLARS AT WORK

A two-hole outhouse in the Delaware Water Gap National Park cost more to build than most homes in 1998. The cost, estimates of which ranged from $333,000 to $450,000, included a 29-inch-thick foundation built to withstand earthquakes, a $13,000 composting toilet, and wildflowers surrounding the cabin sowed at more than $720 a pound. Planning and design alone ate up almost one third of the total cost. Construction itself (outside the $80,000 supervisor's salary) was around $200,000.

A 1997 *Seattle Times* investigation turned up the fact that the cost was not that out of line for similar Park Service projects, thanks to stringent agency requirements (acres of paperwork; all work done to metric specs; a supervisor flown in from Denver). However, a Seattle congressman was shocked to see the results of an appropriations bill he had pushed through, not knowing that "improvements" requested by the Park Service included such a plush pot.

....

In the Ivory Coast of Africa, brands of toilet paper are named for popular American soap operas. You can clean up with Dallas Jumbo or Santa Barbara brand papers.

....

Bathrooms in the executive suites at the Four Seasons Hualalai, Hawaii, made the Travel Channel's list of Most Outrageous Bathrooms partly for the shower stalls made entirely of costly black volcanic lava rock available in their $3,000-per-night suites.

THE MODERN SKYSCRAPER PRESENTS GREAT CHALLENGES TO PLUMBERS

The most obvious problem in building a skyscraper bathroom is getting all that water into the sky. In an ordinary building, street pressure will get water only four or five stories up. The solution is to place a series of pumps and tanks at various levels; each tank supplies the floors directly below it. Chicago's Sears Tower, for example, has tanks in the basement, on the 31st floor, on the 64th floor, on the 88th floor, and on the floor just below the roof.

If getting the water up is the central challenge, getting it safely back down raises its own hurdles. For one thing, wastewater tends to contain a lot of gases, which must be vented. And if the air beneath the water doesn't disperse efficiently, you get a "glug" effect when you flush. To contend with this, plumbers cut vent pipes into the soil stacks at regular intervals.

Finally, piped water can reach a maximum speed of 10 to 20 feet (3–6 m) per second. Fifty floors' worth of office workers can create too much water, which will fall too rapidly. The answer is to build horizontal offsets into the pipe structure, periodically slowing down the flow. The end result is a complicated web of pipes and tanks hidden within the building.

Marilyn Monroe takes a bubble bath in Billy Wilder's 1955 comedy *The Seven Year Itch*.

NOT JUST A MYTH

Rats actually *can* climb into your toilet, if your toilet is at ground level or in the basement. Rats are infamously agile crawlers, but even they can't climb a vertical sewage pipe. It's too slick at the edges for them to negotiate and, at 6 inches (15 cm) in diameter, too wide for them to "chimney." On the other hand, rats are accomplished swimmers, and they have been known to stroll along a horizontal pipe, paddle through the water-filled piping in the toilet, and emerge in the porcelain bowl. If there is a rat in your toilet bowl, however, it's likely that it made its way into the bathroom through a hole in the floor or a vent to the roof, then jumped in for a drink.

SAFETY FIRST!

All bathroom electrical outlets should come equipped with GFCIs (ground-fault circuit interrupters), which switch off power to an outlet if a power imbalance occurs. With the possible collision of electrical appliances and water in a bathroom, GFCIs can reduce the risk of injury.

To prevent scalding in the shower, install a mechanical scald-guard device that shuts off the water if the temperature rises too high. More elaborate electronic temperature-gauge systems do the same thing but without shutting off the water; they automatically adjust the temperature if water flow in some other part of the house affects the shower.

AT THE 1996 INTERNATIONAL SYMPOSIUM ON
PUBLIC TOILETS, HELD IN HONG KONG:

- India's citizens produce more than 237 million gallons (900 million l) of urine and 300 million pounds (135 million kg) of fecal matter per day. Two thirds of the Indian people do not have sewage facilities.
- Mughal (Mogul) kings in India created lavish bathing facilities in the 1500s but reserved them for only the richest citizens.
- The first separate men's and women's toilet facilities were put up at a large Paris party in 1739.
- French authorities in the 1870s asked that public facilities be made available for passersby on the ground floors of buildings. The Palais Royal Hotel in Paris started charging its regular diners a monthly fee for use of the facilities.
- Successive improvements were made to the flushing toilet (first promulgated by John Harrington in 1596) by J. F. Brondel (1738); Alexander Cummings (1775); Joseph Preiser (1777); Joseph Bramah (1778); and S. S. Helior (1870).
- Dr. Pathak himself founded a pay toilet company called Sulabh International in 1970; today, more than 10 million people use his facilities every day throughout India.

Roman officials prevented would-be graffiti artists from defiling public bath walls by painting murals of gods and goddesses on the walls.

AMERICANS AND TOILET PAPER USE:

- 69 percent call it the modern convenience "most taken for granted," topping zippers and frozen food.
- 49 percent chose T.P. over food as the product they would most like to take if stranded on an island.
- 40 percent of people fold or stack T.P. before use, 40 percent wad or crumple, and 20 percent wrap it around their hand. Men are more likely to be folders, while women more often prefer wadding it up.

French entertainer Joseph Pujol (who performed under the stage name Le Petomane, a moniker later used by Mel Brooks's character in 1974's *Blazing Saddles*) could demonstrate more than 30 different kinds of farts and could blow out a candle several feet away with his efforts.

Sign seen in Tokyo streets and subways during the run-up to the 1964 Tokyo Olympics: "Let us all stop urinating in the streets!"

For many years *Chase's Annual Events*, a British reference book, marked January 17 as Thomas Crapper Day to commemorate his death in 1910. Researchers for the International Thomas Crapper Society, however, found that the day should be January 27, Crapper's actual death date.

HISTORICAL HIGHLIGHTS

- Remains of sitting-type toilet facilities have been unearthed in what is today Ahmedabad, India, dating back to 2500 B.C. Similar facilities dating 400 years later were found in Egypt.
- Roman public toilets, benches with keyhole-shaped openings, were sometimes built over flowing streams.
- Greek parties often were interrupted by servants bringing in silver pee pots, which were used communally in public.

....

Medieval English midwives claimed to be able to predict a child's future by examining his or her first stool. Punjabi grandmothers sometimes ate the first excrement of a male child.

....

HE COULDN'T JUST TAKE A DROP?

From *Golf Digest*, this cautionary tale for professional golfers with a certain urge: "Scott Laycock learned a lesson in his first PGA Tournament. Playing in the 2003 Sony Open in Hawaii, he received a two-stroke penalty for riding in a golf cart while searching for a bathroom. Laycock was on the second tee when nature called. The nearest bathroom was a hike away, and Laycock didn't think he would make it, so he accepted a ride in a golf cart. Players are not permitted to ride in carts during tournament rounds unless it is an emergency. Tour official Mike Shea thought that because Laycock did not have diarrhea, this did not qualify as an emergency, and he was penalized. 'That did give me [diarrhea],' Laycock joked."

New Delhi is the home of the Sulabh International Museum of Toilets.

....

**PUBLIC WARNING POSTED BY
THE BRITISH ROYAL COURT IN 1589**

"Let no one, whoever he may be, before, at, or after meals, early or late, foul the staircases, corridors, or closets with urine or other filth."

....

Q What's in feces?

A Food material that could not be digested, water, salts, mucus, cellular debris from the intestines, bacteria, and cellulose fiber. Dead red blood cells create the brownish color. Several diseases can alter the color of stool. Thank the following compounds, among others, for creating the substance's unique and well-known smell: indole, skatole, mercaptans, hydrogen sulfide, and ammonia.

....

The U.S. Department of Energy recommends a temperature of 115°F (46°C) as the proper setting on your home's water heater to prevent your water from becoming dangerously hot.

At the opening of the Neville Public Museum "Privy to the Past" bathroom history exhibit, Green Bay Mayor Paul Jadin tore the first square off of a 7 x 5 foot (18 x 13 cm), two-ply roll of toilet paper billed as the "world's largest." The roll weighed 2,000 pounds (907 kg) and was the equivalent of 10,561 rolls, or 2,207,000 square sheets.

....

GET YOUR MESSAGE ACROSS
Preparations for the 2002 World Summit on Sustainable Development in Johannesburg included the naming of the official toilet paper. Each square on the roll sported a friendly sentiment such as "Hygiene is not a soft issue," and "A flush is not the only winning hand."

....

Tile makers now offer a process by which any favorite photo or artwork can be glazed to a tile for use in your bathroom.

....

A SURVEY BY THE SCOTT PAPER COMPANY REVEALED THAT BY A

★ **2-to-1 MARGIN,** ★

HUSBANDS WERE BLAMED FOR ALLOWING
THE TOILET PAPER TO RUN OUT.

....

The average American home keeps eight rolls of toilet paper on hand as back-up.

A BRIEF HISTORY OF TOILET PAPER, FROM INDIVIDUAL SHEETS TO THE TWO-PLY ROLLS WE KNOW AND LOVE

Joseph Gayetty is credited with inventing what we know as toilet paper in 1857. His "Therapeutic Paper" contained aloe and was sold in packs of 500 flat sheets for 50 cents. Great Britain's Walter Alcock later put it on a roll for the first time in 1879. Like Gayetty, his creation failed to catch the public's interest, what with so many free toilet-wiping products at hand; bathroom users didn't feel the urge to spend money on the stuff.

In 1890, however, the Scott Paper Company put toilet paper on a roll, perforated it for easy removal, and an industry was born. At first, the company only produced private-label paper; that is, merchants bought products with their name on it from the Scott Company. In 1902, the company began marketing its own paper under the trade name "Waldorf."

In 1915, the Scott Company began using a "Fourdrinier" machine that spit out paper 148 inches (3.8 m) wide at 500 feet (152 m) per minute. The rolls were then cut down to 4-inch (10 cm) widths that came in 650- or 1,000-square lengths. By 1925, Scott sold more toilet paper than any other company.

In 1942, St. Andrew's Paper Mill in London saved the world years of agony by inventing and mass-producing soft, two-ply paper. All Scott paper and similar products until that time were single ply.

In 2001, Kimberly-Clark put out the first premoistened, disposable toilet paper, called "Rollwipes." The product, which required a special dispenser that attached to existing roller units, failed to catch on in any great numbers. Movie director Barry Sonnenfeld and actor Will Smith have been quoted as being great proponents of moistened toilet pads.

BEFORE THERE WERE WINGS . . .

Kimberly-Clark Company sold tons of "creped wadding paper" for a wide variety of uses. During World War I, cotton was in such short supply that the company had to develop a thinner form of the product, which they dubbed Cellucotton (see page 40). First used as a filter in gas masks and for bandages, nurses found that it worked perfectly as a sanitary pad. Prior to this innovation, women's sanitary cloths were diaper-like contraptions that were washed and reused. In 1920, Cellu-naps became the first popular, mass-produced disposable sanitary napkin, made of Cellucotton and covered with gauze. (Johnson & Johnson had tried to sell a similar model in the 1890s, but the morals of the day so hampered their advertising and sale that the product was shelved.) Kimberly-Clark soon changed the name of Cellu-naps to Kotex. They sold 12 napkins for 60 cents. Sales were poor until Montgomery Ward put the product in their catalogs in 1926, after which the product found a permanent place in many women's lives.

U.S. military forces used toilet paper to help camouflage their tanks during the first Gulf War.

PUTTING IN A VANITY CABINET AROUND YOUR SINK?
HERE ARE FOUR TYPES OF SINKS YOU'LL HAVE TO CHOOSE FROM:

- **Self-rimming sink** (the rim overlaps the opening in the top of the vanity)
- **Flush-mount sink** (this sink lies flush with the tile top of the vanity)
- **Above-counter basin** (somewhat stylish and a bit retro, these are bowl-like basins that rest completely on top of the vanity)
- **Under-counter mount** (the top of the sink is slightly below the surface of the vanity top)

....

Two-ply toilet paper is made from two layers of No. 10 paper (a measurement of thickness). One-ply is a single layer of thicker No. 13 paper.

....

Standard-size toilet paper comes in squares that are 4.5 inches (11 cm) on each side. Some brands, however, cheat a bit by making slightly narrower or shorter rolls, so consumers are warned to check their package labels carefully.

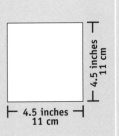

A jumbo roll of toilet paper has more than 1,500 sheets per roll (consumer sizes come in 500 or 1,000 sheets per roll). Jumbo sizes, which require a larger dispenser, are good for public restrooms.

THE AVERAGE TOILET PAPER ROLL WEIGHS

8 OUNCES | **227 GRAMS,**
INCLUDING THE TUBE.

The American Forest and Paper Association estimates that more than 16 billion pounds (15 trillion kg) of tissue-grade paper are produced in the United States each year. This includes toilet and facial tissue, paper napkins and towels, diapers, and other sanitary products.

Hypoallergenic **means that the product contains no inks, dyes, or perfumes that are likely to bring on an allergic reaction in a user.**

According to Charmin, the average roll of toilet paper lasts five days in the most-used bathroom in a household. On average, a person uses 8.6 sheets per trip, 57 sheets per day, and 20,805 sheets per year.

PUBLIC RESTROOM FEARS
(BASED ON A SURVEY OF 1,000 PEOPLE BY KIMBERLY-CLARK):

Percent	Fear
70	Dirty, unsanitary conditions
10	Contracting germs
8	Bad odor
5	Sharing with "strangers"
2	Dislike quality of paper products
1	Watery hand soap

The electronic faucets now seen regularly in public bathrooms (the ones where you put your hands under the faucet and an electric eye automatically turns on the water) are moving into new residential construction. The key difference is that users can adjust the temperature of home versions.

ONE CORD OF WOOD WILL YIELD

1,000 POUNDS (454 KG) OF TOILET PAPER	7.5 MILLION TOOTHPICKS	460,000 PERSONAL CHECKS

Georgia-Pacific gives this description for why toilet paper is soft: During the drying process of the paper-making procedure, the toilet paper sheet is adhered to a large steel cylinder to dry. It is then scraped (or "creped") off by a metal blade. Creping imparts flexibility and stretch in the sheet, while lowering the strength and density, resulting in soft tissue products.

U.S. NAVY SHAVING REGULATIONS

NAVY PERSONNEL REGULATIONS [NAVPERS] 56651
Chapter 2, Section 2
Article 2201.2

Shaving and Mustaches (Men). The face shall be clean-shaven unless a shaving waiver is issued by the commanding officer. . . . Mustaches are authorized but must be neatly and closely trimmed. No portion of the mustache shall extend below the lip line of the upper lip. It shall not go beyond a horizontal line extending across the corners of the mouth and not more than $1/4$ inch (0.6 cm) beyond a vertical line drawn from the corner of the mouth. The length of an individual mustache hair fully extended shall not exceed $1/2$ inch (1.3 cm).

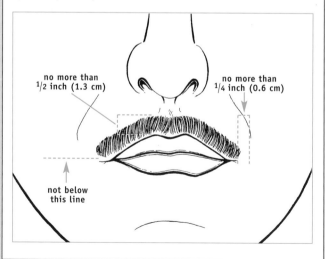

no more than $1/2$ inch (1.3 cm)

no more than $1/4$ inch (0.6 cm)

not below this line

Dr. West's Miracle-Tuft Toothbrush was released in 1938 by DuPont as the first such product made with synthetic bristles.

....

One package of Maybelline's Great Lash Mascara is sold every 1.9 seconds worldwide.

....

A Swedish company is working to perfect a system that would dispense reading material—newspaper pages, magazine articles, etc.—printed on toilet paper so one could read, use, and flush.

....

Bathroom Remodeling for Dummies **offers this tip:**
"Don't put any form of lighting within reach
of someone in a bathtub or shower."
Thanks . . . good idea.

....

THE UNITED STATES USES ABOUT

4.8 BILLION GALLONS | **18** BILLION LITERS

OF WATER EVERY DAY TO FLUSH WASTE.

....

The straight razor met its match beginning in 1847, with the invention of the "hoe-style" razor by William Henson of England. It looked like modern shavers of today, with a T-shape.

Percent	Frustration Factor
33	Empty dispenser
23	Tissue breaks off too quickly
12	When rolls sit on top of tank
11	When tissue hangs off roll onto floor

The Charmin company first used a baby in its toilet paper ads in 1953, when the Charmin Baby took the place of the Charmin Lady. In 1964, Mr. "Please don't squeeze the Charmin" Whipple made his first appearance on TV and radio. The character was created by the Benton & Bowles advertising agency and took his name from the then-president of the ad firm. Former vaudeville actor Dick Wilson played Mr. Whipple on TV for more than 20 years. By the 1970s, Mr. Whipple's name was the third most-recognized name in the United States, trailing only President Richard Nixon and evangelist Billy Graham.

TOP HONORS

The National Kitchen and Bath Association (Hackettstown, New Jersey) includes a Hall of Fame. The Hall "honors individuals who have made extraordinary contributions to the kitchen and bath industry as a whole." Inductees include faucet pioneer Al Moen, Roy Jacuzzi (who invented it), and Herbert Kohler Jr. of the Kohler bathroom fixture company.

SAY ALOHA TO T.P.

During the energy crisis of the mid-1970s, everyday supplies were slow to arrive in faraway Hawaii due to high fuel costs. Along with long lines at gas stations, Hawaiian consumers faced shelves nearly devoid of a wide variety of paper products, including toilet paper. Many store owners kept toilet paper behind their counters, rationing out one roll per person per visit.

....

I talian and French dentists in the 1840s, inspired by a discovery by dentists in Naples, suggested that patients suck on lozenges made with fluoride and honey to avoid tooth decay.

....

OUR HOPES FOR THE FUTURE OF ★ PUBLIC ★ RESTROOMS
(BASED ON A SURVEY BY KIMBERLY-CLARK)

- Voice-activated product dispensers
- Music
- Full-time bathroom attendants
- Telephones in every stall
- Modem lines/electrical outlets in stalls

....

B.Y.O.T.P.

For 10 years, bathrooms in Heritage Junior High in Detroit did not provide toilet paper. A 1986 toilet paper ban aimed at reducing student vandalism lasted until 1996.

KEY INTERNATIONAL
TOILET PAPER BRAND NAMES

Bulgaria: Belana
Canada: Kruger
Egypt: Flora
Finland: Embo
France: Lotus Bath Tissue
Germany: AB Grigiskes
Greece: Elle and Delica
Hungary: Crepto and Szilvia
Ireland: Kittensoft

Italy: Tenderly
Japan: Fukoyo, Yame Seishi, and Poppy Seishi
South Africa: Nampak and Carlton
Spain: Colhager Bathroom Tissue
Thailand: Sit and Smile
Turkey: Selpak
United Kingdom: Andrex

Bridal showers boast a different use for toilet paper. Teams of attendees dress one member of their team in a bridal gown made of nothing but toilet paper, with the bride-to-be choosing the winning team's handiwork.

United Kingdom annual toilet paper sales:

600 MILLION ROLLS OR **APPROXIMATELY 10 ROLLS PER PERSON.**

Ivory Soap, the first soap to float, was invented by accident in 1878. Too much air entered a batch of soap being made at Procter and Gamble's soapworks in Cincinnati. The resulting bars became popular so fast that P&G swung into action to make Ivory their number one product.

The Petit Lutin brand of toilet paper sold in France comes printed with a different bit of information on every sheet. Readings include sayings, geographical trivia, or small artistic images.

ESTIMATES OF TOILET PAPER USE IN CHINA EXCEED

5.6 BILLION POUNDS | **2.6 BILLION KILOGRAMS**

——— ANNUALLY ———

Toilet paper in Taiwan is often sold in packages of sheets rather than rolls.

YOU LOOK LIKE DEATH!

Arsenic Complexion Wafers were sold in the eighteenth century to help fashion-savvy chewers achieve that longed-for ghostly pallor. Of course, they were also actually poisoning themselves.

A male Chinese tourist spread the SARS virus in Hong Kong in early 2003 while visiting his brother. The man, who had diarrhea, used the bathroom at his brother's apartment, and water droplets were spread throughout the apartment building by ventilation fans, according to Hong Kong health secretary Dr. Yeoh Eng-kiong.

A BUBBLY BROOK!

Before 1965, detergents in sewage sometimes caused surface foam on rivers and streams. Most laundry detergents contained a substance called alkylbenzene sulfonate (ABS), which did not break down completely in sewage treatment systems. In 1965, after more than 10 years of research, the detergent industry developed linear alkylbenzene sulfonate (LAS). Bacteria quickly break down LAS molecules, so detergents that contain LAS do not cause foam. Rivers everywhere breathed a less-strangled sigh of relief.

....

After the passage of a 1994 U.S. law mandating low-flush toilets, the Libertarian Party spoke up. "Politicians who claim the era of big government is over are busy regulating the volume of water in our toilets. Talk about being bowled over by government intervention!" said national party chairman Steve Dasbach.

In 2000, Rep. Joseph Knollenberg tried to have the provision repealed, but his bill failed to pass. "Let's take politics out of the bathroom," he said. "Regulating the size of America's flush is none of Washington's business. . . . Nowhere in the Constitution does it give the federal government authority over the size of our flush."

....

ART IMITATES LIFE

In 1917, artist Marcel Duchamp shocked the art world by presenting a urinal as art. Though mocked at the time, it remains a touchstone in the debate over "what is art." A reproduction of the piece was sold by Sotheby's in 1999 for $1.76 million.

Airplane toilets work with a vacuum system. The waste is sucked down into the sewage receptacle, accompanied by approximately a half-gallon of blue disinfecting fluid. No water is used or kept in the bowl to prevent it from escaping into the cabins during flight. The urban legends of "blue ice"—chunks of frozen blue airplane passenger waste—are mostly true. Chunks do occasionally fall off of airplanes when on-board receptacles are full and overflow.

PRACTICE MAKES PERFECT

The book *Going Abroad* recommends practicing your aim in your home bowl before traveling to areas of the world where squat toilets are in use. To do this, place blocks of wood on either side of your bowl and place your feet on them so that you are squatting above the toilet. Or else dig a hole in your (fenced-in, please) backyard and practice there.

By a margin of more than **four to one**, people **older than 50** prefer to have the toilet paper hung with the loose end over the top rather than from underneath.

Bismuth, the key ingredient in several stomach ailment remedies, was first noted in literature by the German monk Basil Valentine in 1540. Pepto-Bismol is the most popular bismuth-based product; it debuted in 1919.

FROM **SAVEYOURSMILE.COM,** —— SOME TIPS ON **DENTAL CARE**

- It takes two to three minutes to carefully brush all the surfaces of your teeth and gums.
- Brushing without flossing is like washing 70 percent of your body in a bath and leaving the other 30 percent dirty. Flossing removes bacteria that can grow between teeth and add to decay and other health problems.
- Brushing the tongue can help eliminate odor-causing bacteria.
- Clean as far back on your tongue as you can without gagging.
- A dry mouth is a great place for bacteria to grow; keep yourself hydrated by drinking plenty of water.
- Mouthwashes that contain chlorine dioxide are the best for removing bacteria.
- Sugarless gum helps stimulate saliva, which helps clean the mouth of sulfur compounds.

....

You can't usually smell your own breath by cupping your hand over your mouth and sniffing (though it seems to work okay in the morning when odors have had all night to stew). We usually don't send out bad breath fumes unless we're talking. The worst breath is found at the back of the throat, and this is forced out when one is talking, especially for long periods of time.

WHAT IS ALL THAT STUFF IN TOOTHPASTE?

HERE'S A RUNDOWN OF SOME OF THE INGREDIENTS FOUND IN POPULAR BRANDS:

- **Aluminum oxide** is an abrasive that helps clean teeth.
- **Blue 1 and yellow 5** are among several names for colorings added to various brands.
- **Calcium peroxide** is an antiseptic and provides oxygen to teeth.
- **Carnuba wax** gives toothpaste texture.
- **Carrageenan,** from seaweed, contributes to its pasty texture.
- **Hydrogen peroxide** helps whiten teeth; it's the active ingredient in bleaching kits.
- **Pentasodium triphosphate** cleans and adds to the texture of the paste.
- **Poloxamer 407** is a detergent-like cleanser; it also helps form toothpaste gels.
- **Polyethylene glycol** is a substance that binds the materials of toothpaste together.
- **Propylene glycol** prevents toothpaste from hardening in the tube.
- **Sodium bicarbonate** (baking soda) is a mild abrasive that removes plaque; similar substances such as silica and calcium carbonate also can be used.
- **Sodium carbonate** cleans teeth and neutralizes acids.
- **Sodium fluoride** and **sodium monofluorphosphate** add cavity-preventing and tooth-strengthening fluoride.
- **Sodium pyrophosphate** prevents the formation of plaque when used regularly; it is often found in tartar-control toothpaste.
- **Sorbital** is a chemical that makes toothpaste taste sweeter and prevents hardening.
- **Tetrasodium pyrophosphate** helps clean the teeth.
- **Titanium dioxide** is a white pigment that colors the paste.

A *lota* is a small pitcher-like object used in Pakistan for cleaning oneself after using an indoor, nonflushing toilet.

GET ON THE BUS!
Some cities in Thailand and other Asian countries use toilet buses. They are parked in busy areas and decorated with palms and other potted plants.

Some monasteries located on high cliffs in Bhutan have small rooms attached to the outside of the walls. These rooms contain toilet holes that empty into the air and the rocks far, far below.

At the Union Hotel in San Juan Bautista, California, visitors can see (but not use) a two-story outhouse built in the 1800s.

Many Bhutanese houses are two-story affairs. The lower story is where household animals live and it is also where the toilet empties, providing additional feed for the animals.

POTTY TRAINING ON THE ROAD
In Shanghai, some streets provide gratings placed at strategic places in the sidewalk near the gutters. Parents working on toilet-training their youngsters can take advantage of these handy toilets.

In a 2004 *San Francisco Examiner* article, Dr. Scott Hyver noted that microorganisms can't live long on toilet seats, but he recommended using the paper covers—just in case.

A 1928 survey revealed that more than **20 million** Americans still did not have indoor bathrooms in their homes (about **17 percent** of the total population).

A Swiss company manufactures the Hygolet. With each flush, a new plastic sheath slides over the seat, while the old cover slides into a receptacle underneath.

EVERYBODY LOOK AWAY
Travelers on the polar ice cap quickly realize that the vast and featureless landscape provides no cover for relieving oneself. One traveler noted that at the beginning of their long journey by ski, trekkers walked far away from camp to go. As the trip progressed, bathroom trips became shorter and shorter. Darkness could not cover these mini-treks either, as the South Pole was in 24-hour sunshine.

SOAP IS MADE USING
ONE OF TWO DIFFERENT PROCESSES:

Kettle method: Steel tanks hold mixes of fats (vegetable oils or animal fats) and alkalis (most often sodium hydroxide). Heating the mixture for several hours causes saponification (also called hydrolysis). Salt is added, and the "neat soap" rises to the top. This substance is put into a device called a crutcher, and perfumes, germicides, and other additives are mixed in. The mix can then be hardened into bars.

Continuous processing: Producing much more soap in less time, this method uses a steel tube called a hydrolyzer, which can be as tall as 80 feet (24 m) but is only 3 feet (0.9 m) in diameter. Hot, pressurized water mixes with hot fats. The fatty acids are split in this process and then removed and mixed in a hydrolyzer with alkali to make the soap. As in the kettle method, the mixture then goes into the crutcher to be hardened into bars. Other continuous machinery sprays hot liquid "neat soap" into a vacuum chamber, where excess moisture and impurities are removed from the soap. Then the dried soap is cut into the shape of noodles and fed into one or two kneading units. Perfume is added to the soap, which comes out of the units in a long bar called a log.

B efore World War I, the U.S. Health Department, in an effort to expand the availability of sanitary bathrooms in rural areas, cheaply sold plans for a can toilet, which was basically a canister with a hole in the top and a cover for the hole. These creations helped popularize the slang expression for the bathroom: "the can."

BIGGER WAS BETTER IN ANCIENT ROME

Several Roman baths were enormous in size. The Baths of Caracalla were more than 1,100 square feet (102 sq. m) and could hold more than 1,500 bathers at one time. The Baths of Diocletian were also immense. They were so large that the vestibule alone was large enough that its site today holds an entire church building, the church of Santa Maria degli Angeli in Rome.

....

In some Southeast Asian nations, water, rather than toilet paper, is more often used to wash after using the facilities. In *Going Abroad*, Eva Newman reports that she saw rolls of toilet paper displayed in colorful containers on restaurant tables in lieu of napkins.

....

More than **220 miles (354 km)** of aqueducts supplied Rome in the first century, though only **30 miles** of them ran above ground. Romans used **300 gallons (1,136 l)** of water per person per day (much of that in fountains, however). By that time, according to one accounting, Rome itself had **11 public baths** and **856 private baths**. By A.D. **315**, Rome also boasted **144 public latrines**.

In a Roman bath, after water was poured over the subject by attendants, they were scraped by a small curved instrument called a *strigil*. Soap, not yet in wide use, was not part of the ritual.

I RUB-A-DUB THEE . . .

Today, Queen Elizabeth honors various well-known British citizens by naming them to the Order of the Bath. The original knights of this order (begun in 1399) earned the name literally. As they reclined in a bath (probably with cold water only), older knights came and "informed, instructed, and counseled" them in the order's traditions and chivalry. Other bathing, drying, and dressing rituals were part of the ceremony. Today's honorees do not even get wet.

Great Britain's Worshipful Company of Plumbers, a kind of proto-trade union, was formed in 1610 by the order of King James I.

The ancient Roman love of bathing traveled with them throughout their empire. A fort near Hadrian's Wall in Great Britain boasted a bathhouse, latrines, water tanks, and a tap for flushing water through the system. The pipes were clay or wooden and sometimes held in place by iron hoops.

TIPS FOR SHAVING THEIR HEAD

- A multiple-blade razor is recommended.
- Avoid shaving against the grain; shave in the direction your hair grows (or used to grow).
- The absolute best way to shave your head is to ask your partner to do it.
- If you choose to use chemical hair-removers, make sure you follow directions. Leaving these products on too long can cause irritation.

....

An anonymous writer described the late seventeenth century activities at Bath, England, a place named, not surprisingly, after its large royal and public baths: "Here is perform'd all the Wanton Dalliances imaginable; celebrated Beauties, Panting Breasts, and Curious Shapes, almost Expos'd to Publick View; Languishing Eyes, Darting Killing Glances, Tempting Amorous Postures, attended by soft Musick, enough to provoke a Vestal to forbidden Pleasure, captivate a Saint, and charm a Jove."

....

Now a sought-after rarity, "The Bathrooms Are Coming" was an early-'70s album of songs celebrating "the glory of custom bathrooms."

....

The name *Pine-Sol* is actually short for "pine solvent." Lysol comes from "lye solvent," and was first introduced to the United States from Germany in the 1890s.

THE POWER OF A GOOD SOAK
A British sanitarium opened in 1765 boasting both cold and hot water baths. These therapeutic baths were used for calming patients rather than for cleaning patients or staff.

....

The British Public Baths and Wash Houses Act of 1846 encouraged more washing by citizens. By 1870, several dozen bathhouses had opened, but bathing was still far from common.

....

A 1958 reference book claimed that
42.4 MILLION
American homes owned
television sets.

Only
41
MILLION
had bathtubs.

....

The world's fastest barber, according to the *Guinness Book of World Records*, is Denny Rowe of England, who shaved 1,994 men in an hour with a disposable razor on June 19, 1988. No word on the record for nicks and cuts.

....

THIS HOLE IS "JUST RIGHT"
An out-of-use three-hole privy in Somerset, England, features three holes of differing sizes, perhaps for use by a family with children in the early twentieth century.

SOMEONE'S GOT TO DO IT

In London in the early nineteenth century, four-men crews called "nightmen" cleaned out public toilets by lamplight. The holeman would fill a tub with waste from the cesspool, climbing down a ladder to reach the stuff. The ropeman raised the bucket to the top of the hole. Two tubmen used a wooden pole to raise and carry the bucket and empty it into a cart. Every town and city in England had several such crews, who were paid to remove the waste and also profited by selling the "nightsoil" to farmers.

....

Alexander Cummings patented a "water closet" in 1775, which featured for the first time a U-bend in the drain pipe to help prevent odors from rising back through the pipe between uses. Water remained in the bottom of the U after each flush.

....

In 1859, the Reverend Henry Moule popularized an "Earth toilet" in which dirt was stored below the toilet hole. Waste mixed with the soil and was periodically turned, removed, then used as compost. Variations on the basic Earth toilet model employed rotating canisters of dirt that emptied after each use.

....

A company called Haywire Productions sells figurative and abstract art printed on stickers that are designed to affix to standard-size toilet seat covers or toilet tanks.

RESULTS FROM AN ONGOING UNIVERSITY OF ALBERTA BATHROOM HABITS SURVEY:

Action	Percent of Respondents
Wipe while sitting	77
Wipe after standing	23
Inspect paper after wiping	76
Don't look	24
Double-dip*	40
Don't double-dip	60
Hang paper over top	79
Hang paper from bottom	21
Always wash hands afterward	45
Sometimes wash hands	44
Never wash	9

*Fold paper and rewipe

....

At www.icbe.org, visitors can join the many online forums discussing various aspects of life in the public toilet arena. That's right, the International Center for Bathroom Etiquette is the place to go if you need to know which urinal to use (never the middle one), whether to use your cell phone or not while in the toilet (not), what is the proper "angle of incidence to avoid splashback" (various solutions are offered), and whether to hang the paper over or under (the debate rages).

....

A 2002 directive for the U.S. Army allowed enlisted people to go completely bald, whether naturally or by choice, reflecting the growing popularity of the "bald look."

THE TOP 10 URINALS IN THE WORLD

AS CHOSEN BY THE AUTHORS OF URINAL.NET, AN ONLINE GALLERY OF PHOTOS OF URINALS FROM DOZENS OF COUNTRIES

1. Amundsen-Scott South Pole Station

2. Hong Kong Sheraton Hotel and Towers

3. Public restrooms of Rothesay (Scotland)

4. The Millennium Dome (London)

5. Women's urinal at Dairy Queen (Port Charlotte, Florida)

6. The Felix (restaurant, Hong Kong)

7. International Space Station

8. John Michael Kohler Arts Center (Sheboygan, Wisconsin)

9. Madonna Inn (San Luis Obispo, California)

10. TV Hill (Kabul, Afghanistan)

At Rothesay, visitors enjoy working Victorian-era plumbing and beautiful black marble fixtures; the granite urinals in the Felix face a floor-to-ceiling window overlooking Kowloon Harbor, providing users with a spectacular view; the Kohler center is the home of the bathroom fixtures manufacturer, and each urinal (and most of the toilets in the building) are covered on all surfaces with original art created especially for the space; at the Madonna Inn, a rock wall serves as the target, and the breaking of a beam of light by one's stream activates the waterfall along the wall that serves as a flush; atop TV Hill in Kabul, soldiers use simple pipes sticking out of the ground, but the view while using them is of Kabul in the background and a minefield in the foreground.

A SURVEY BY A SHOWER GLASS MANUFACTURER ELICITED THE FOLLOWING RESULTS:

When asked whom they would most like to find in their shower, **39 percent** of men and **40 percent** of women answered their significant other. (Men also voted for Demi Moore, Jennifer Aniston, and Britney Spears in large numbers.) The survey also showed that **31 percent** of men and **24 percent** of women brush their teeth while showering. **Fifteen percent** of men and **14 percent** of women will leave the shower to answer the phone. A surprise (to us, at least) was that more than **53 percent** of each gender chose a relaxing shower over a spot of television as the way to unwind after a hectic day.

In Australia, it is not unusual to see toilets that allow for little or big flushes. Buttons are provided for each level of flushing.

KEEPING IT ALL FLOWING

The key part of the modern toilet is the bowl siphon, the hole in the bowl that keeps the water level but through which all the water leaves when the bowl is flushed. The flush happens because the water level rises up quickly enough to flood the siphon tube, which then sucks all the water out at once. Try this: Add water to the bowl a cup at a time and nothing happens. Add water with a bucket, and you get a flush. When the handle is pushed down, that sudden onrush of water from the tank causes the flush.

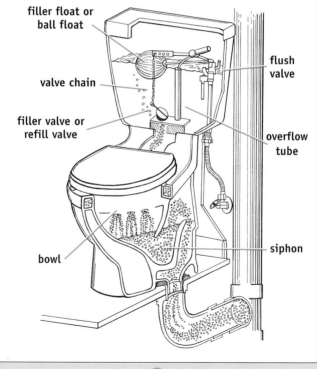

filler float or ball float

valve chain

filler valve or refill valve

flush valve

overflow tube

bowl

siphon

HOLD IT! NOW SMILE!

Toiletnet.com features hundreds of photos of toilets from around the world and sells an annual wall calendar featuring photos from its collections. Included are photos from (mostly American) airports, bars, churches, casinos, gas stations, several U.S. Navy vessels, parks, schools, private homes, baseball stadiums, and other places. There are also photos of the bathrooms and toilets at the Jimmy Carter Presidential Center (the urinals there use no water), the Royal Ontario Museum, and the Alamo. The photos are often referred to as "toilaroids."

....

All my good reading, you might say, was done in the toilet.
—Henry Miller, in *A Saturday Afternoon*

....

Styptic pencils are used to fix small shaving cuts. The aluminum sulfate that is the main ingredient of the sticks causes quick clotting of the blood, which stops the bleeding.

....

RAW TOILET POWER

In 2004, both the Kohler Company and American Standard announced new toilet models that boasted a larger-than-normal opening at the bottom of the tank. The holes, which are more than 3 inches (7.5 cm) wide, claim the companies, increase flow and help prevent clogs. Kohler says that its Cimarron model is "inspired by the raw power of class five whitewater rapids." As the *Los Angeles Times* wrote, "Some solutions seem so obvious."

Plumbers in Florida and other states report that, if they are open on the day after Thanksgiving, business is up "more than 60 percent" over regular days.

....

BY 2003, ANNUAL SALES OF TOILET PAPER HAD TOPPED **$19 BILLION WORLDWIDE**

....

Urinals in the home are rising slightly in popularity, thanks to larger bathrooms and a little publicity. Ozzy Osbourne and NFL star Curtis Martin both showed off their in-home models on television programs. An article from November 2003 reported that more and more men had convinced their wives to have one installed. Very large bathrooms sometimes have separate wings for the man and woman of the house, making the addition of a urinal less noticeable.

....

HAIR CONDITIONERS APPLIED AFTER SHAMPOOING WORK IN THE FOLLOWING WAY:
They coat strands of hair, smoothing over small scales that make up the shaft of the hair itself. The smoothing action creates more elasticity in the hair and reduces breakage. All this adds up to shinier, bouncier hair.

....

Most toilets flush on an E-flat note.

{ELVIS PRESLEY}
He's all soaped up.

THE FIVE
MOST LUXURIOUS BATHROOMS
AT RESORTS AROUND THE WORLD:

- Four Seasons Resort, Hualalai, Hawaii
- Caesars Pocono Resort, Paradise Stream, Pennsylvania
- Cap Juluca, Anguilla
- Anse Chastanet Resort, St. Lucia
- Maroma Resort & Spa, Riviera Maya, Mexico

Those seeking to put a little Victorian flair into their bathrooms can choose to install such items as the Sunrise Victorian pull-chain water closet, offered by Vintage Tub and Bath for only $1,175.

GREEN MEANS "GO"
Middle-of-the-night bathroom-goers can thank an Arcadia, California, company for inventing the LavNav, a light placed on the underside of the lid of the toilet. A motion sensor detects movement and turns the light on, with a red light indicating that the seat is down and a green light indicating that the seat is up.

More than **325,000** urinals are made in the United States each year.

New York's Mandarin Oriental Hotel in Manhattan boasts that most of its suites' bathrooms sport stunning views of either the Hudson River to the west or Central Park to the east.

The bathroom scale knows nothing
of extenuating circumstances.
—Mason Cooley

LOS ANGELES MAGAZINE RAN DOWN THESE EXAMPLES OF ACTRESS-SINGER JENNIFER LOPEZ'S ALLEGED "BATHROOM FIXATION":

- When attending a baseball game with Ben Affleck, she had a stadium bathroom "roped off for privacy."
- Affleck allegedly designed a jewel-inlaid toilet seat for her.
- She supposedly had Affleck deliver "softer" toilet paper to her during a visit to a Starbucks in Beverly Hills.
- Her first husband claimed that he was not allowed to use her bathroom because of her fear of germs.

When using a squat toilet, empty your pants pockets before squatting above the hole in the floor. This prevents objects from falling into the toilet.

- Widen the doorway to 36 inches (0.9 m).
- If you can't widen the door, use special hinges that allow the door to open wider, away from the jamb.
- Make sure doors open into hallways, away from the bathroom. Should you fall in the bathroom, the door could easily be opened by someone outside.
- A pedestal-style sink allows wheelchairs to roll underneath more easily.
- Pads or blocks under the toilet seat can raise it to a higher level for easier access.
- Recessed, vapor-proof, GFCI-equipped lights placed in the shower can make showers brighter.

....

One of the hottest trends in new bathroom construction has been the addition of heated floors. Electrically heated wires or hot-water pipes are installed beneath tile or linoleum. Towel warmers are also growing in popularity.

....

The Hansgrohe Raindance 240 sports a 10-inch (25 cm) diameter shower head that is claimed to accurately mimic the feel of rain, with a center hole that "aspirates air through the shower head." Bring your umbrella.

There is a room that no self-respecting householder can do without, and that is the bathroom.
—H. R. Jennings in 1902

....

BUILDING A BETTER TOILET

American Standard's proprietary "Flush Tower" (a departure from the typical ball-and-chain) is powerful enough to remove up to 29 golf balls (standing in for waste) in one flush, according to company testing.

....

SOME OPINIONS GLEANED FROM A 2001 SURVEY OF OFFICE WORKERS:

83% say their home bathroom is cleaner than their work bathroom

47% think about work while in the office loo

27% think about after-work activities

10% think about lunch

84% are against unisex bathrooms

2% admit to writing on bathroom walls

The Ritz-Carlton New York, overlooking Central Park, offers a unique hotel service: the bath butler. Call ahead and have a hot or warm scented bath awaiting your arrival, along with a tubside snack.

A 1996 SURVEY OF FEMALE ELEMENTARY SCHOOL TEACHERS REVEALED THAT:

10% brought her entire class to the bathroom with her

50% avoided drinking fluids during the school day

5% used pads or adult diapers

In 1998, the Occupational Safety and Health Administration issued a directive to employers to ensure that employees not only had adequate bathroom facilities, but that they were actually allowed to use them. It read in part, "employees can use them when they need to do so" and stated that employers "may not impose unreasonable restrictions on employee use of the facilities."

The Great American Ballpark in Cincinnati, one of the newest parks in baseball, opened in 2003 with 507 water closets, 240 urinals, and 509 sinks. There are 77 showers in the two locker rooms.

The American Hotel & Lodging Association Educational Institute offers a wordless 30-minute video used to train new luxury hotel cleaning staff. Using only demonstrations, graphics, and sound effects, the video skips over the language barrier and shows how to leave a hotel room, especially a bathroom, spick and span. An alternate version is available for economy hotels.

....

ANCIENT ROMAN SHAVING FACTS

- Around 300 B.C., a young man's first shave, at the age of 21, was a moment of great celebration and partying.
- When Scipio Africanus, conqueror of Hannibal, showed up clean shaven in 202 B.C., the fashion swept the city.
- However, when the Emperor Hadrian (circa A.D. 100) grew a mighty beard (allegedly to hide a bad complexion), shaving was suddenly out of favor with Roman men.

....

A special haircut helped William the Conqueror overcome the Saxons who inhabited England in 1066. Shaving their heads to look like monks, William's advance spies went undiscovered by the Saxon soldiers.

....

THE LAW OF SUPPLY AND DEMAND

During Women's National Basketball Association games at the Staples Center in Los Angeles, about 75 percent of the men's rooms are relabeled to become women's rooms, reflecting the high female attendance at the games. Male fans are thus heard to grumble about how far they have to walk to find facilities.

SINK STYLES

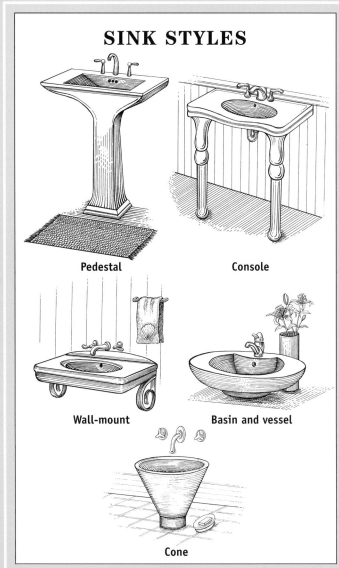

Pedestal

Console

Wall-mount

Basin and vessel

Cone

TREND-SETTING STYLE

The practice of women shaving their armpit hair was not widespread until the Wilkinson Company, makers of shaving devices, devised a radical publicity campaign. The May 1915 issue of *Harper's Bazaar* showed a model wearing an evening gown that exposed her shaved armpits. Within two years, sales of razor blades doubled.

....

Bald inventor Todd Greene debuted the HeadBlade in 1999. Winner of several design awards, the razor's wide head and easy-grip handle are designed specifically for shaving heads. Unlike regular razors, the HeadBlade is pushed rather than pulled across the scalp. The company also sells HeadSlick, shaving cream designed for use on the head. The HeadBlade has received dozens of mentions in international men's magazines.

....

TWO ARE BETTER THAN ONE

Inventor Herbie McNinch created a Y-shaped, two-headed razor in 1995. According to McNinch, the two heads, each containing two blades, are designed to give "twice the shave in half the time."

....

The Twyford Versatile Interactive Pan uses special detectors to analyze a patient's waste products to provide diagnostic information to the person's doctor. The data can be sent via email from the device or broadcast over a small speaker. Voice-recognition software helps distinguish registered users from unregistered ones.

1. Assemble tools: rags, toilet brush, abrasive sponge, grout brush, etc.

2. Strip the room, removing all towels; check the curtain for mildew.

3. Spray disinfectant; leave the room and let the product do its stuff.

4. Return to the bathroom and scrub all surfaces with a short-handled brush. Start with the shower walls and work down. Use a toilet brush on the inside of the bowl.

5. Rinse the washed surfaces; use the shower spray to rinse the shower and tub. Use a wet sponge on counters and sink.

6. Shine any metal surfaces with a soapy cloth or special bathroom cleaner spray.

7. Put out clean towels; replace toilet paper as necessary. (This is when they create those neat little triangles.)

8. Spray and wipe the floor, using cloths, a mop, or a vacuum cleaner as necessary.

9. Allow the room to air dry.

A Cornell University study found that "cleanliness of the bathroom" finished number one among qualities most desired by hotel guests.

Essel Propack, based in Mumbai, India, makes more than 3.5 billion toothpaste tubes each year, including those used by Crest. The company uses a process that forms seven layers of plastics into the tubes. The tubes used to be made with aluminum, but, as Essel CEO Cyrus Bagwadia told *Forbes* magazine, "Aluminum tends to leach, and it needs a lot of washing. Fluoride, for example, reacts with aluminum to form a toxic chemical. And some of the solvents used in processing aluminum can contaminate what is inside." Also plastic and metal-laminated tubes "are cleaner, and they can be decorated more easily than metal tubes."

CAN YOU SPARE A SQUARE?

In a 2001 survey of office workers, researchers found that 81 percent of those surveyed said they would "provide bathroom tissue to a person next to them" in the event there was none in their stall. Ten percent said they would do so only if they knew the other person.

A tale is told of a very religious Jewish man who fell into his London privy pit one Saturday in about 1250. Out of respect for the Sabbath, he refused help in getting out. By the time he was rescued a day later, he was too ill to recover.

COTTON MANUFACTURERS DEFINE THESE FIVE TYPES OF TOWELS:

- **Terry:** Woven on a loom, using an additional yarn to form loops on both sides of the towel (called pile or loop surfaces).
- **Printed:** Colorful designs are printed on the surface of either terry or velour towels, normally only on one side.
- **Velour (or Sheared):** Produced in the same fashion as terry, but with an additional process that cuts the terry loops on one side. The terry side should face the skin for optimum drying.
- **Jacquard:** Either terry or velour, these patterned towels have a design woven right into them that is constructed on a special type of loom.
- **Embellished:** Some manufacturers add embroidery or lace to a towel as a decorative element.

On August 28, 2003, the Holiday Inn chain of hotels held their first-ever Towel Amnesty Day, on which they asked light-fingered guests to return towels taken ("borrowed") from the hotels. The hotel promised that the towels would be received without penalty to the thief/guest. Guests were asked to share their stories about why they took towels on the company's Web site. Total returns were not announced, but some reports cited "thousands." (Holiday Inn donated $1 per towel to a children's charity.) The 25 best on-line stories earned the submitters a limited-edition souvenir towel . . . that did not have to be returned to the hotel.

The diary of the stationmaster at Wolferton Royal Railway Station, near Norfolk, England, records that from 1898 to 1907, the kings of Portugal, Spain, and Greece visited the station and while there, used the royal urinal.

St. Catherine of Siena, trying to shore up her piety, not only never washed, but practiced a form of self-denial that had her avoid defecation for long periods.

In medieval England, workers known as *gongfermors* (or rakers) carried away accumulated piles of human waste.

Cloacina was the Roman goddess of sewers.

British sanitary engineer George Jennings did his utmost to spread the emerging gospel of the toilet in the mid-1800s. He created public toilet facilities for cities in England, as well as in Buenos Aires, Cape Town, Madrid, Frankfurt, and Sydney. Among his innovations was the circular urinal tower, with urinals arrayed around a central pillar that supplied water to each receptacle. With the support of the Prince of Wales, Jennings urged more attention be paid to simple washing as a means to slow the spread of various diseases.

A 1929 book titled *Color and Style in Bathroom Furnishing and Decoration* was called the "first book ever devoted to the bathroom as a subject of interior decoration." Until then, bathroom design had been the interest of designers and their wealthy clients. But this book was aimed at a more down-to-earth clientele and offered reasonably priced ways to make a bathroom more than just a place to do your business.

The global market for cosmetics is estimated to be more than **$60 BILLION ANNUALLY.**

TOP TUBES

Since 1968, the Tube Council, founded as the Collapsible Tube Manufacturers' Association in 1914, has presented the Ted Klein Tube of the Year award to a company with the best tube-packaged product. Awards are also given in various other categories. Tubes are judged "on the basis of general consumer sales appeal of the tube package, including graphics, closure, shape, texture, and ease of use. The most innovative tube was judged on decoration, graphics, finish, closure, innovation of the content, and overall technical merits." The 2002 Ted Klein Award winner was Victoria's Secret's Rapture Golden Pearl Shower Cream. The Innovative Tube of the Year award went to TIGI for its BedHead Dumb Blonde Reconstructor.

BREAKDOWN ★ OF THE ★ COSMETICS MARKET IN THE U.S.

Company	Share of Market
L'Oreal	21.2
Estée Lauder	19.6
Procter and Gamble	13.0
Others	46.2

In Victorian times, some makers of ceramic urinals included a small painting of a bee on the walls of the urinal. The Latin for bee is "apis."

According to *Time*, sales of Maybelline products outside the United States grew **93 percent** from **1996 to 2002.**

Sales of men's grooming products in Great Britain topped **$1.5 billion** in **2003.**

Irish chamber pots sometimes came adorned with a picture of British prime minister William Gladstone so that users could express patriotic sentiments every time they used them.

THE FIRST LINES OF COLORED BATHROOM FIXTURES. AMONG THE COLORS OFFERED:

- Ivoire de Medici (white)
- Ming Green
- Orchid of Vincennes (violet)
- Ionian Black
- Meissen White
- Royal Copenhagen Blue
- St. Porchaire Brown
- T'ang Red
- Claire de Lune Blue
- Rose du Barry

The first commercial passenger airplane with a bathroom began flying in 1919.

I'M AWFULLY FOND OF YOU

"Rubber Duckie," perhaps the most famous bathroom song, was written for *Sesame Street* by Emmy-winning composer Jeffrey Moss. The character Ernie first sang it on the show in 1970. It actually reached as high as No. 16 on the pop charts that year.

The Kohler Company's first bathtub was a horse trough/hog scalder to which John Michael Kohler applied baked enamel coating. Troughs eventually gave way to more stylized bathtubs.

In 1927, revolutionary American designer and engineer Buckminster Fuller created 4D House, using entirely innovative design and construction. One feature was the "Five by Five" or "Dymaxion" bathroom. The prefab unit covered only 25 square feet (2.3 sq. m), and all fixtures and piping, including the stamped aluminum walls, weighed only 420 pounds (191 kg). The four parts of the bathroom were simply bolted together and hooked to a water supply.

From **1900 to 1932**, more than **350 inventors** of various forms of water closet applied to the U.S. Patent Office to register their innovations.

The Chinese of the middle of the first millennium A.D. were among the first to popularize paper, and they are recorded as among the first to employ toilet paper.

A new father quickly learns that his child invariably comes to the bathroom at precisely the times when he's in there, as if he needed company. The only way for this father to be certain of bathroom privacy is to shave at the gas station.
—Bill Cosby

Romans are well known for their use of public baths, but they're not the only ones with a commitment to cleanliness. Similar baths were also used throughout the Middle Ages by residents of the Islamic Empire as well as areas of China.

....

According to abcnews.com, actress Susan Sarandon displays her Oscar statuettes in her bathroom.

....

I test my bath before I sit
And I'm always moved to wonderment
That what chills the finger not a bit
Is so frigid upon the fundament.
—Ogden Nash, 1942

....

The toilet paper that inevitably escapes trash piles created by intrepid mountaineers on various Himalayan peaks is sometimes referred to as "white man's prayer flags" by the local Sherpas, a reference to the Buddhist practice of flying (unsoiled) bright orange, red, or yellow flags.

....

In 2004, the Gillette Co. spent approximately
$4.5 million
on commercials that aired during
Super Bowl XXXVIII.

A survey revealed that 68 percent of Americans prefer over the top, with 25 percent preferring the underneath method. Seven percent have no preference.

OVER THE TOP
Pros
- Allows hotel maids to make those nice triangle things after they finish cleaning.
- Easier to grab.
- More traditional.
- Easier to tear off if dispenser has a "tear-bar."

Cons
- More people touch more of the roll, perhaps by brushing their fingers against it as they pull off their final sheets, thus increasing contamination.

UNDERNEATH
Pros
- Less cross-contamination from others, as you don't touch the roll when removing sheets. If the paper is dangling down flush with the wall, one need not come close to the rest of the roll when extracting sheets.
- Easier and less awkward to remove when toilet area is a very small space.

Cons
- Makes traditionalists angry (very angry).
- Sometimes hard to grab when it adheres slightly to wall.

AUTHOR'S NOTE
AND ACKNOWLEDGMENTS

When I started looking into writing and compiling this book, I quickly realized that many people had gone before me, so to speak. I was somewhat stunned to discover just how fascinated many people are with bathrooms (and toilets in particular). The British and Japansese seem positively entranced by their loos.

Bathrooms are that rare thing that unites humanity. From the loftiest president or king to the most humble worker bee, no one can escape a visit to some form of a bathroom. So, I hope you have enjoyed this world-spanning peek into the most universal of rooms.

The information in this bathroom companion was gathered and synthesized from many sources. The list that follows includes a few of the more significant resources, though there were dozens of others. My thanks to all of them and my apologies if I got anything wrong. Thanks also to writers Phil Barber and Jim Gigliotti for their research help and to Mark Shulman for helping out with a few.

To my readers, enjoy this in good health . . . and eat your roughage.

SOURCES

The Bathroom, by Alexander Kira (Bantam, 1966)

Bathroom Stuff, by Holman Wang (Sourcebooks, 2001)

Bogs, Baths, and Basins: The Story of Domestic Sanitation, by David Eveleigh (Sutton Publishing, 2002)

Clean & Decent: The Fascinating History of the Bathroom and the Water-Closet, by Lawrence Wright (Penguin, 1966)

Going Abroad, by Eva Newman (Marlor Press, 1997)

The Porcelain God: A Social History of the Toilet, by Julie L. Horan (Carol Publishing, 1996)

www.americanstandard.com

www.dentalreference.com

www.kohler.com

www.plumbingworld.com

www.theplumber.com

www.toiletology.com

www.toiletpaperworld.com

PHOTOGRAPHY AND ILLUSTRATION CREDITS